Social Studies Alive!®

Methods to Transform Elementary Instruction

Chief Executive Officer: Bert Bower

Chief Operating Officer: Amy Larson

Director of Product Development: Liz Russell

Managing Editor: Laura Alavosus

Project Editor: Ava Hayes

Production Manager: Lynn Sanchez

Design Manager: John F. Kelly

Graphic Designer: Victoria Philp

Photographer: Tim Stephenson

Contributing Writers: Sherry Owens, Lisa West

Teacher Consultants: Leslie L. Frizzell, Kristi L. Grubaugh

Teachers' Curriculum Institute
P.O. Box 1327
Rancho Cordova, CA 95741

Customer Service: 800-497-6138
www.teachtci.com

ISBN 978-1-58371-112-5
3 4 5 6 7 8 9 10 -EBM- 15 14

Introduction

In a lower-elementary activity, students discover what a map is and learn to use its basic features. Here they are physically moving from square to square to see how a map grid works.

Elementary school teachers across the nation face the challenge of teaching a standards-based social studies curriculum. In some states, social studies has joined reading, writing, and math on the high-stakes standardized tests. Holding schools responsible for measuring student mastery of social studies concepts has focused welcome attention on the place of social students in the overall school curriculum. However, many elementary teachers feel unprepared to teach this subject. In an effort to be sure they are covering all the material required by the standards, teachers may fall back on a straight textbook approach—read the chapter, answer the questions at the end—with the unfortunate result that too many students find social studies boring.

Is the standards movement really at odds with engaging, dynamic instruction? At Teachers' Curriculum Institute (TCI), we don't believe this is an either-or proposition. Our years of classroom experience have shown that when social studies is taught through an active, student-centered approach, students do learn and remember important content. We have created a teaching approach that is mindful of the challenges of standards-based instruction, yet also genuinely excites students about social studies. We call it the TCI Approach, and it is the basis of the *Social Studies Alive!* core program for the elementary school.

A New Approach to Teaching Elementary Social Studies

The TCI Approach had its roots in the 1980s. As a small group of middle and high school history teachers, we began experimenting with innovative instructional methods and found that they generated unprecedented enthusiasm among our students. Weaving together educational research and theory with the realities of classroom teaching, we developed the *History Alive!* program, based on the series of instructional practices that now define the TCI Approach. Some years later we met with a group of elementary teachers from across the nation and asked, "Do you think the educational theories and teaching strategies behind the *History Alive!* approach would work at the elementary level?" Their answer: "Absolutely!"

That was the beginning of a partnership that led to the development and publication of *Social Studies Alive!* This K–5 series of curricular materials, which enables students with diverse learning styles to "experience" social studies, has helped elementary teachers nationwide revitalize their social studies programs. As a result, students are entering middle and high school social studies classes better prepared. They are also improving their reading comprehension, writing ability, critical thinking, and standardized test scores. And they are becoming more excited than ever about social studies.

In an upper-elementary activity, students "act out" projected images of farm scenes from different eras. In this way, they experience the dramatic changes in farm life over the last 200 years.

Why Is It Important to Teach Social Studies?

There is no shortage of voices explaining why teaching social studies at the elementary level is vital. Here are three:

- "When children are empowered by knowledgeable and skillful teachers with the ideas, skills, values, questions, and attitudes that compose the social studies curriculum, their *judgment* is improved. Consequently, they can reason historically, help solve community problems, appreciate diversity, protect the environment, and, with deep understanding, empathize with the hopes, dreams, and struggles of people everywhere." (Parker, *Social Studies in Elementary Education,* 2001.)

- "At the early elementary level, government can be described as the people and groups within a society with the authority to make, carry out, and enforce laws and to manage the disputes about them. These fundamental ideas about government and its functions provide a basis on which children in their earliest school years can begin to develop an understanding of the formal and informal institutions and processes of government in their communities, states, and the nation." (The Center for Civic Education, *National Standards of Civics and Government,* 1997)

- "The purpose of social studies for young children, K–6, as for all age groups, is to enable them to understand and participate effectively in their world. Social studies explains their relationship to other people, to institutions, and to the environment. It equips them with the knowledge and understanding of the past necessary for coping with the present and planning for the future. It provides them with the skills for productive problem solving and decision making, as well as for assessing issues and making thoughtful value judgments. Above all, it integrates these skills and understandings into a framework for responsible citizen participation, whether in their play group, the school, the community, or the world." (National Council for the Social Studies, *Standards and Position Statements,* 1984)

"A child miseducated is a child lost."

—John F. Kennedy

These three rationales are only a sampling of the thousands of pages written about the purposes, goals, and standards of elementary social studies education in our multicultural, global, and increasingly interconnected society. To these, we would add the relatively simple, straightforward rationale underlying the *Social Studies Alive!* program: Learning about social studies is fun. Elementary students are inherently fascinated by the world around them and are eager to understand and be a part of that world.

Social Studies Alive! lessons capture this excitement by creating real-life experiences for students to learn from. As you implement the TCI Approach, the engaging lessons will energize both you and your students. Soon you will claim social studies as a vital part of your teaching day.

The TCI Approach

The TCI Approach consists of a series of instructional practices that allows students of all abilities to experience key social studies concepts.

Theory- and Research-Based Active Instruction

Lessons and activities are based on five well-established theories:

1 **Multiple Intelligences**—According to Howard Gardner's revolutionary theory, every student is intelligent—just not in the same way. Because everyone learns in a different way, the best activities tap more than one kind of intelligence. Gardner has described these seven intelligences: verbal-linguistic, logical-mathematical, visual-spatial, body-kinesthetic, musical-rhythmic, interpersonal, and intrapersonal.

2 **Cooperative Interaction**—Elizabeth Cohen's research has led her to conclude that cooperative groupwork leads to learning gains and to higher student achievement. Cohen has found that if students are trained in cooperative behaviors, placed in mixed-ability groups, and assigned roles to complete during a multiple-ability task, they tend to interact more equally. This increased student interaction leads to more learning and greater content retention.

3 **Spiral Curriculum**—Educational theorist Jerome Bruner championed the idea of the spiral curriculum, in which students learn progressively more difficult concepts through a process of step-by-step discovery. With this approach, all students can learn once a teacher has shown them how to think and discover knowledge for themselves.

4 **Understanding by Design**—Grant Wiggins and Jay McTighe believe that teaching for deep understanding requires planning backward—first determining the big ideas students are to learn and then working backward to identify methods to reach those goals and ways to assess the effectiveness of teaching.

5 **Nonlinguistic Representation**—Many psychologists believe that we think and remember better when we store information in both linguistic and nonlinguistic forms. Research by Robert Marzano and colleagues demonstrates that teaching with nonlinguistic activities such as graphic organizers, mental images, and movement helps to improve students' understanding of content.

Standards-Based Content

Dynamic lessons build mastery of state and national social studies standards. Integrates hands-on active learning, achieving a consistent pattern of high quality social studies instruction while being mindful of standards.

Preview Assignment

A short, engaging assignment at the start of each lesson helps you preview key concepts and tap students' prior knowledge and personal experience.

Multiple Intelligences Teaching Strategies

Multiple Intelligence Teaching Strategies incorporate six types of activities:

1 **Visual Discovery**—Students view, touch, interpret, and bring to life compelling images, turning what is usually a passive, teacher-centered activity—lecturing—into a dynamic, participative experience.

2 **Social Studies Skill Builder**—This strategy turns the traditional, rote tasks usually associated with skill-based worksheets into more dynamic, interactive activities.

Experiential Exercise—These short, memorable activities make abstract ideas or remote events accessible and meaningful by tapping into intrapersonal and body-kinesthetic intelligences.

Writing for Understanding—These activities give all learners, even those with lesser linguistic skills, something memorable to write about.

5 **Response Groups**—This strategy helps students grapple with the ambiguities of issues in social studies, recognize the complexity of historical events, and discuss the consequences of public policies.

6 **Problem Solving Groupwork**—This strategy teaches students the skills necessary to work together successfully in small groups, both in the classroom and later in life.

Considerate Text

Carefully structured reading materials enable students at all levels to understand what they read. Recognizes that a successful reading of expository text involves four stages: previewing the content, reading, taking notes, and processing the content or reviewing and applying what has been learned.

Graphically Organized Reading Notes

Comprehensive graphic organizers used to record key ideas, further help students obtain meaning from what they read. Graphic organizers help students see the underlying logic and interconnections among concepts by improving their comprehension and retention in the subject area.

Processing Assignment

An end-of-lesson processing assignment, involving multiple intelligences and higher-order thinking skills, challenges students to apply what they learned. Helps students synthesize and apply the information they have learned in a variety of creative ways.

Assessments to Inform Instruction

Carefully designed tests encourage students to use their various intelligences to demonstrate their understanding of key concepts while preparing them for standardized tests.

Why Use the TCI Approach?

"I love this program. It not only has helped to motivate my students' learning but has made me more reflective as a teacher. I have even found myself using the strategies in my language arts and reading classes."

Some of the teaching methods inherent in the TCI Approach will require that you make changes in the way you teach. Why should you risk change? Here are some of the reasons given by teachers who use the TCI Approach.

Teachers need innovative, practical alternatives to conventional social studies teaching. Most teachers have discovered that conventional teaching methods reach fewer and fewer students each year. They need ways to reach students that are dynamic yet practical. The TCI Approach provides an effective alternative to the traditional, teacher-centered classroom.

Teachers need ways to help students see how social studies concepts, past and present, are connected to their world. Students forget much of what they learn in social studies classes because they have no way to apply that knowledge. Teachers need to convey the many ways in which social studies concepts affect students' lives today—in the use and abuse of power, discrimination, democratic involvement, the value of social services, and human use of the environment.
For example, a lesson involving case studies of people who have solved environmental problems in and around their communities, followed by an exploration of environmental problems close to home, gives students an understanding of the real ways they can contribute to a better world. When students are continually challenged to apply their social studies knowledge to the world around them, they are well on their way to becoming lifelong learners.

In an elementary activity, students pilot an imaginary space shuttle from outer space to their landing site on Earth, learning to identify geographic features in the process.

Teachers need guidance on how to create a supportive learning environment. Urging students to take risks, praising them for their attempts, and treating mistakes and "failures" as learning opportunities can create a supportive learning environment. The result is more cooperative, tolerant behavior.

To use their critical thinking skills, students need to become active learners. Students best learn social studies by involvement: leading, acting, singing, discussing, drawing, making their own decisions, presenting, and critiquing others' work. In such active tasks, students must apply new knowledge as they solve a problem, analyze a situation, understand a perspective, or evaluate alternatives. This type of thinking engages their higher-order intellectual skills.

Students must be responsible for their own learning. Challenging students to create a product (a poster, an advertisement, a poem, a written dialogue, a journal, a timeline) or a presentation (a panel discussion, a dramatization, an oral report) allows them to "own" the learning process. The result is a high level of involvement and follow-through on class activities

"Social studies is my favorite class because we do fun things. We don't just read a textbook — instead we get to do an activity that helps me remember things. I wish every teacher taught social studies this way."

Students need more time to work together. Rather than having students work individually at their seats, teachers need to foster student interaction with peers, which teaches vital social skills and leads to learning gains.

Teachers who are sensitive to issues of multiculturalism need realistic ways to teach social studies from a variety of perspectives. Teaching from a multicultural perspective, and stressing that the differences among races, nations, and ethnic cultures are at least as profound and as durable as the similarities, helps students learn to appreciate and navigate those differences in their increasingly globalized world.

Teachers need to nurture their zest for teaching. Most teachers enter the profession with a sense of purpose: to reach the unreachable student, to create a better future by educating the leaders of tomorrow. The stressful reality of school life, however, dims many a teacher's initial optimism. Teachers using the TCI Approach often report a renewed sense of idealism as they rediscover the mission and the enjoyment they first associated with teaching. They find they are reaching all their students, not just the "best," and they report that this is the way they always wanted to teach—with a sense of purpose, passion, and fun.

How Does *Social Studies Alive!* Help Teachers?

Some elementary teachers are apprehensive about teaching social studies, perhaps because they lack a strong social studies background or are wary of increasing their workload. However, the elementary educators who created *Social Studies Alive!* took several steps to ensure that the program supports teachers' efforts:

- The program comes with all the materials you need: student text, teacher lesson guides, audio CD, transparencies, placards, student handouts, Interactive Student Notebooks, assessments, and Interactive Desk Maps.
- There is a comprehensive lesson guide for every grade level. These guides have won universal praise from elementary teachers as being readable, easy to follow, and time-saving.
- Each lesson is divided into short teaching segments designed to fit easily into available time slots. At the lower-elementary level, segments may take 10 to 20 minutes; at the upper-elementary level, 15 to 45 minutes.
- Every lesson comes with the detailed background information you need to teach concepts in history, economics, civics, and geography.

Social Studies Alive! is a carefully designed and thoughtfully sequenced program. This hands-on, minds-on approach requires an energetic and committed teacher. We can assure you that your commitment to active, meaningful social studies instruction, in combination with the ideas of the TCI Approach, will lead to truly inspired teaching and learning.

"I feel that anything that inspires a desire for knowledge can only improve a student's reading and writing skills. The activities and strategies in this program give students a desire to read on, find out, and write creatively."

What You Can Expect from This Book

The purpose of this methods book, *Social Studies Alive! Methods to Transform Elementary Instruction,* is to convey a clear picture of the instructional practices that characterize the TCI Approach at the elementary level and to provide some practical tools for implementing those practices.

Part 1 explores the features of the TCI Approach. It discusses the theoretical basis for the approach, describes the steps for using each of six multiple intelligence teaching strategies, and shows how to support students' growth in reading. **Part 2** explains the process for creating a cooperative, tolerant environment in your classroom—a key to your success with all other parts of the TCI Approach. **Part 3** gives you tips on using the Interactive Student Notebook as an engaging way for students to organize information and to explore what social studies means to them.

Each part of the book takes into account the needs and perspectives of two groups of potential users: (1) those of you who are completely new to the TCI Approach and would like to learn more, either about using *Social Studies Alive!* or about adapting the general approach to design powerful, multiple-intelligence lessons that support any curriculum, and (2) those of you who are already using *Social Studies Alive!* and want to strengthen your lesson presentations with creative ideas that get immediate classroom results. For both groups, the book is chockfull of practical instructional tips and strategies, supported by examples from TCI's core elementary program. Whether you are participating in a professional development workshop or reading this book in another context, you will learn how to offer more active, meaningful instruction in an energized, revitalized classroom.

"I have been using Social Studies Alive! strategies for three years, and the responses from my students have been everything I could have hoped for and more. I have seen delight, interest, curiosity, surprise, and amazement. My students have been pushed, challenged, frustrated, and tested—and they have loved every minute of it."

PART

1

The Elements of the TCI Approach

Theory- and Research-Based Active Instruction

Yes! They are highly diverse, but according to the theory of multiple intelligences, every student is intelligent—just not in the same way.

The TCI Approach was developed by teachers who sought to combine what they had learned from classroom experience with the accepted wisdom of educational theory and research. From years of working with students, these teachers observed that when kids are active, they stay focused, are more motivated, and learn better. Thus, "active learning" was an essential ingredient of their emerging approach. To this foundation, they added ideas drawn from Howard Gardner's theory of multiple intelligences, Elizabeth Cohen's research on cooperative groupwork, Jerome Bruner's spiral curriculum, Grant Wiggins' and Jay McTighe's understanding by design, and Robert Marzano's nonlinguistic representation. Educational theory, then, contributed the five key premises behind the TCI Approach: (1) students learn best through multiple intelligences, (2) cooperative interaction increases learning, (3) all students can learn via the spiral curriculum, (4) students benefit from having explicit learning goals, and (5) learning is optimized when linguistic and nonlinguistic experiences are valued equally.

The Theory of Multiple Intelligences

The typical classroom contains a broad range of abilities. In a fifth-grade classroom, Michael reads at the seventh-grade level, while Kayla struggles with a third-grade book; Alexis responds to writing prompts at a level acceptable to a middle school teacher, while Tony writes at a second-grade level; Carlos articulates his thoughts clearly, while Victoria hardly says a word. Many elementary educators have confronted this challenge by placing students in leveled ability groups. However, this type of academic tracking poses a fundamental dilemma. A crucial goal of social studies education is to prepare students for effective participation in a pluralistic society, yet policies that separate students from one another according to academic ability also tend to separate them by social class, race, and language.

"With the three premises built into all the lessons and activities, what was once a dusty, dry area of learning for most teachers and students is now fresh, exciting, and engaging."

Academic segregation sends students a clear message: equal participation and cooperation by diverse groups in society is possible in theory only. Learning theorists and psychologists, however, have proposed an alternative concept of intelligence that abandons the outdated practice of academic tracking.

Howard Gardner, a neuropsychologist at Harvard University, argues that we must develop a new way of looking at human intelligence:

> "In my view, if we are to encompass adequately the realm of human cognition, it is necessary to include a far wider and more universal set of competencies than has ordinarily been considered. And it is necessary to remain open to the possibility that many—if not most—of these competencies do not lend themselves to measurement by standard verbal methods, which rely heavily on a blend of logical and linguistic abilities. With such considerations in mind, I have formulated a definition of what I call an 'intelligence.' An intelligence is the ability to solve problems, or to create products, that are valued within one or more cultural settings." (Gardner 1993, p. x)

According to the theory of multiple intelligences, a student may struggle with logical thinking, yet have a strong interpersonal intelligence. Teachers need to use activities that tap all students' strengths.

These students are using their body-kinesthetic intelligence as they recreate the relative population densities of urban, suburban, and rural communities.

Gardner relies on neurological research to argue that the human mind has at least seven relatively autonomous human intellectual competencies, each with its own distinctive mode of thinking, to approach problems and create products. (Gardner has more recently identified an eighth intelligence, and is investigating at least one other.) The TCI Approach supports the following seven intelligences described by Gardner:

"I don't like to just sit in my seat all day. I do better when my teacher lets us move around and act things out. Those are the things I remember."

- **Linguistic intelligence** is responsible for the production of language and all the complex possibilities that follow, including poetry, humor, storytelling, grammar, metaphors, similes, abstract reasoning, symbolic thinking, impromptu speaking, oral debate, conceptual patterning, and all genres of the written word. Linguistic intelligence is awakened by the spoken word; by reading someone's ideas or poetry; by writing one's own ideas, thoughts, or poetry; and by listening to a speaker or a group discussion.

- **Logical-mathematical intelligence** is most often associated with what is called scientific thinking or deductive reasoning: the ability to observe and understand details as part of a general pattern. Inductive thought processes are also involved, such as the ability to make objective observations, and, from the observed data, to draw conclusions, to make judgments, and to formulate hypotheses. Logical-mathematical intelligence involves the capacity to recognize patterns, to work with abstract symbols, and to discern relationships and perceive connections.

- **Visual-spatial intelligence** deals with such things as the visual arts (including painting, drawing, and sculpting), navigation, mapmaking, and architecture, all of which involve physical awareness and the use of space. Games such as chess and marbles, which require the ability to visualize objects from different perspectives and angles, also are included. The key sensory base of this intelligence is the sense of sight, but the ability to form images and pictures in the mind is also involved.
- **Body-kinesthetic intelligence** is the ability to use the body to express emotion (as in dance and body language), to play a game (as in sports), or to create a new product (an invention). Learning by doing has long been recognized as an important part of education. Our bodies know things our minds don't and can't know in any other way. Actors, clowns, and mimes demonstrate the endless possibilities for using the body to know, understand, and communicate in ways that touch the human spirit.

Let Your Students "Feel" Concepts

Few techniques are more powerful for connecting students with important concepts than creating opportunities for them to step into the shoes of relevant figures and react to the issues, passions, and events affecting them.

Musical and intrapersonal intelligences come into play as these students create a public service message that encourages others to learn about cities in the West.

Cognitive Pluralism: More than Buzzwords

Every social studies objective should be taught through as many of the intelligences as possible. This allows for more equitable learning by giving all students access to ideas.

Cooperative groupwork promotes student achievement and productivity. Not only are they learning social studies, but they are reinforcing social skills.

- **Musical-rhythmic intelligence** includes the recognition and use of rhythmic and tonal patterns, as well as sensitivity to sounds in the environment, the human voice, and musical instruments. Of all forms of intelligence identified thus far, musical-rhythmic intelligence has the greatest "consciousness altering" effect on the brain. Music calms you when you are stressed, stimulates you when you are bored, and helps you attain a steady rhythm during such activities as typing and exercising. It has been used to inspire religious beliefs, to intensify national loyalties, and to express great loss or profound joy.
- **Interpersonal intelligence** involves the ability to work cooperatively in a group, and the ability to communicate verbally and nonverbally. It builds on the capacity to notice contrasts in moods, temperament, motivations, and intentions among other people. Those with highly developed interpersonal intelligence can have genuine empathy for another's feelings, fears, anticipations, and beliefs. Counselors, teachers, therapists, politicians, salespeople, and religious leaders usually have strong interpersonal intelligence.
- **Intrapersonal intelligence** involves knowledge of internal aspects of the self, such as feelings, the range of emotional responses, thinking processes, self-reflection, and a sense of (or intuition about) spiritual realities. Intrapersonal intelligence allows you to be conscious of your consciousness. Self-image and the ability to transcend the self are part of the functioning of intrapersonal intelligence.

Cooperative Interaction

The second theoretical premise behind the TCI Approach is easily stated: Cooperative interaction leads to learning gains. Researchers report that cooperative groupwork promotes higher student achievement and productivity than either competitive or individualist teaching methods; the more opportunities students have to interact—by discussing a controversial topic, preparing each other for a quiz, conducting peer interviews—the more they will learn and remember.

However, sociologists have discovered that when students perform a collective task, some are more influential than others. Elizabeth Cohen (1986) has found that students expect certain performances from one another. Students prejudge what their peers will be able to contribute on the basis of perceived academic ability and peer status. As a group, they believe some students are "low status" and others are "high status." When high-status and low-status students work together, a self-fulfilling prophecy results: students perceived as having high-status tend to interpret most of the questions, talk more, and have their opinions accepted more often than do students perceived as low-status. This inequality results in a learning disparity: high-status students, because they interact more, learn more; low-status students, because their interaction is severely limited, learn less.

Virtually every teacher faces the problem of status inequality. Researchers have shown that such inequality exists in every classroom, no matter how homogeneous a classroom may appear (Berger, Rosenholtz, and Zelditch 1980). Unless we acknowledge this problem and deal with it frankly, our efforts to increase student interaction may ultimately backfire if only high-status students reap the benefits.

Fortunately, research has uncovered practical ways to combat the problem. Cohen has found that when teachers use heterogeneous groups and learn how to change expectations for competence, the low-status students participate more and high-status students no longer dominate. Cohen's work has focused exclusively on students working in groups of four or five; the classroom implications of her studies are explored in greater detail in the later discussion of the strategy "Problem Solving Groupwork."

Many of the techniques that Cohen has found effective with small groups can be used with larger groups and with paired instruction. By implementing these ideas in combination with Howard Gardner's theory of multiple intelligences, you can create cooperative interaction. All students in the heterogeneous classroom become convinced that they possess skills that are valued. With the TCI Approach, your activities combat the problem of status inequality by tapping into the multiple intelligences, enabling you to create cooperative interaction that leads to learning gains for all students.

"Groupwork is an effective technique for achieving certain kinds of intellectual and social learning goals. It is a superior technique for conceptual learning, for creative problem solving, and for increasing oral language proficiency."

— Elizabeth Cohen
Professor of Education,
Stanford University

Benjamin Bloom's Taxonomy: A Guide for Creating Questions

Knowledge The ability to recall specifics, universals, methods, processes, and patterns

Comprehension The ability to translate, interpret, and extrapolate

Application The ability to use abstractions in concrete situations

Analysis The ability to analyze elements, relationships, and organization principles

Synthesis The ability to put together elements and parts to form a whole

Evaluation The ability to make judgments about the value of ideas, works, solutions, and methods

To help students analyze an image related to early English settlements in North America, you can lead them to higher-order thinking skills by carefully spiraling your questions from the basic to the complex.

- What do you see?
- Why might people have traveled thousands of miles to settle at Roanoke?
- What challenges might these people have faced?
- What clues in the picture indicate that something might have happened to the people who lived here?
- What would be a good caption for this image?

The Spiral Curriculum in Action

The third theoretical premise behind the TCI Approach is the idea of the spiral curriculum, championed by educational theorist Jerome Bruner in his landmark book *The Process of Education* (1960). Underlying this theory is the belief that all students can learn if a teacher shows them how to think and discover knowledge for themselves. "The quest," according to Bruner, "is to devise materials that will challenge the superior student while not destroying the confidence and will-to-learn of those who are less fortunate." The concept of the spiral curriculum can be applied to individual activities as well as to entire lessons and units.

The idea is to structure lessons carefully to lead students through a step-by-step process of discovery. Students should first explore an event, idea, or personality by using elemental cognitive skills—observation, description, identification, recall—and then spiral to ever-higher levels of cognition such as interpretation, application, and synthesis. This gives all students the cognitive building blocks they need to reach higher-order thinking.

By leading students through this process of discovery, you ensure that students from a variety of academic levels will have the conceptual information they need to answer complex questions. In *Social Studies Alive!* each lesson is designed with the spiral curriculum in mind, carefully orchestrating activities that allow students to move from the simple to the complex and challenge them to use higher-order thinking skills. This approach is highly effective in the heterogeneous classroom and leads all students to a greater understanding and appreciation of social studies.

Understanding by Design

Grant Wiggins and Jay McTighe supply the fourth theoretical component of the TCI Approach: the use of a Big Idea or Essential Question to focus students on an explicit goal. Wiggins and McTighe (*Understanding by Design,* 2005) believe that teaching for deep understanding requires planning backward—first determining the big ideas that students are to learn and then working backward to identify methods to reach those goals and ways to assess the effectiveness of teaching. Planning backward is a three-stage process, according to Wiggins and McTighe. Stage 1, the Desired Results, involves determining what we want students to understand and then turning those understandings into questions. These Essential Questions establish a broader perspective for what students are to learn and be able to do with their learning. Stage 2, the Assessment Evidence, in effect, asks, "If this is what we want students to understand, how will we know that they've grasped it?" This phase deals with figuring out a variety of ways to collect evidence of student understanding—both informal and formal types of assessment. Stage 3, the Learning Plan, identifies the learning activities and instruction to help students reach the stated goals. An effective Learning Plan answers the questions, "How will the design

- help the students know where the unit is going and what is expected?
- help the teacher know where the students are coming from (prior knowledge, interests)?
- hook all students, and hold their interest?
- equip students, help them experience the key ideas and explore the issues?
- provide opportunities to rethink and revise their understandings and work?
- allow students to evaluate their work and its implications?
- be tailored (personalized) to different needs, interests, and abilities ?
- maximize initial and sustained engagement as well as effective learning?

"Theory. Theory. Theory. Teachers always hear theories. But the beauty of this approach is that finally, theory is put into practice. This changes what happens in the classroom."

Nonlinguistic Representation

Finally, the TCI Approach incorporates the premise that we think and remember better when we store information in both linguistic and nonlinguistic forms. Research by Robert Marzano and his colleagues demonstrates that teaching with nonlinguistic activities, such as graphic organizers, mental images, and movement, helps to improve students' understanding and retention of content.

Teaching with nonlinguistic representation helps all students to learn and is an integral part of *Social Studies Alive!* This approach also fits nicely with Gardner's theory of multiple intelligences. Graphic organizers both in the Student Editions and in the Reading Notes of *Social Studies Alive!* are especially helpful to visual-spatial learners. Activities that involve movement, such as human bar graphs, provide memorable experiences for all, and particularly for those who excel in body-kinesthetic intelligence.

Standards-Based Content

Teachers report consistent positive results on standardized test scores after implementing the TCI Approach.

The advent of the standards-based curriculum in social studies has been a mixed blessing. Too often, the emphasis is on coverage over depth, expedience over exploration, memorization over real understanding. Ultimately, this is proving shortsighted. Elementary students are increasingly turned off to social studies, and many enter middle school actively disliking the subject. In such an environment, student performance on standards-based tests is bound to plummet. That's why educators need to find an approach that is mindful of standards but still supports hands-on, active learning, to keep students excited about social studies. This is the goal of the TCI Approach and the *Social Studies Alive!* program.

How Does the TCI Approach Address State and National Standards?

Given that standards-based reform has been driving efforts to improve student achievement across the curriculum, any instructional approach must revolve around the content standards and curriculum frameworks that are being formulated at the district, state, and national levels. *Social Studies Alive!* was carefully designed to meet the elementary standards of the National Council for the Social Studies, as well as the standards for the English language arts sponsored by the National Council for Teachers of English and the International Reading Association. On the TCI Web site (teachtci.com), you will find individual state correlations linked to *Social Studies Alive!* Whether you use TCI's published curricular program or create your own lessons based on the TCI Approach, addressing the standards is fundamental; any use of this methodology falls short unless it also targets the essential content for which students are accountable.

Aligning classroom instruction with academic content standards is working for states with high-stakes testing of social studies standards. Thousands of teachers who have been trained in the TCI Approach have achieved impressive learning gains in both social studies and language arts test scores—and not by "teaching the test." Rather, these teachers kept their focus on a rich curriculum and sound instructional practices. They helped their students experience a "walking tour" through colonial Williamsburg to learn about life in the American colonies. They prompted students to re-create a lively Loyalist/Patriot debate over whether the colonies should declare their independence. They watched as their students staged scenes to represent amendments in the Bill of Rights, and put on skits that reflected the reactions of different groups to westward expansion in the 1800s. Their students' knowledge *and enjoyment* of U.S. history soared, and test scores reflected their success.

"[This TCI program] has completely energized my teachers. The revolutionary approach to teaching encouraged them to work in concert with each other as opposed to the traditional isolation that teachers experience."

In TCI training workshops, teachers are energized as they learn how to teach social studies standards through sound instructional practices. Enthusiastic teachers plus engaged students equals classroom success.

"Build a park... a school... a bike lane." In this lower-elementary activity, children explore how community leaders and citizens interact to make choices about spending community dollars. As this theme recurs through the grade levels, students learn how to participate in political activities and use the democratic process to influence public policy.

Aligning content to state and national standards is only one part of boosting test scores. TCI has discovered another factor that contributes to the mastery of important standards: a consistent pattern of high-quality social studies instruction that is implemented at every grade level.

TCI's published curricula achieve this, offering school districts the nation's first fully articulated, methodological scope and sequence. That is to say, teachers using TCI materials employ the same teaching strategies, adapted to be developmentally appropriate at each grade level, from students' first experience with social studies in kindergarten through their high school courses.

This unique, comprehensive K–12 social studies curriculum is the result of the fruitful collaboration between elementary and secondary teachers that produced *Social Studies Alive!* The elementary teachers were eager to tap into the content expertise of the secondary teachers; the secondary teachers were enthusiastic about finding ways to create a strong elementary foundation in social studies. Together, they wrote, tested, and published this series of elementary lessons that are totally engaging and on target for young students, while employing the same powerful educational theories and teaching strategies that secondary teachers had found successful in their classrooms.

Districts that have implemented TCI programs across all grade levels are seeing great results. Their students enjoy the experience of learning social studies through lessons that are both inviting and memorable. They are getting, even before middle school, foundational concepts in the four main strands of social studies: history, geography, civics, and economics. Thus, they are well prepared for more in-depth studies in middle and high school.

The benefits of this comprehensive approach are many: better coordination between lower-elementary, upper-elementary, middle school, and high school programs; a spiraling approach with careful repetition of key concepts across the grades, which leads to increased retention and application of ideas; and more efficient use of time, since students move from grade to grade both better prepared and already organized to learn.

The ultimate goal of the TCI Approach, then, goes far beyond raising standardized test scores. Our mission is to engage all learners in the diverse classroom so that social studies becomes one of their favorite subjects. In this way, students will not only perform better academically, but will also become lifelong learners. In the world our students will soon inherit, no outcome could be more vital.

In the coming sections, you'll learn precisely how the elements of this dynamic approach work in concert to create learning experiences for students that are relevant, engaging, and memorable.

"I love what [TCI] has done for my students' achievements. Specifically, our group of ESL students raised its scores an incredible 30% with the use of the TCI program. That is a major WOW!"

Preview Assignment

Preview activities are quick and simple. Students record responses to short, engaging assignments in their Interactive Student Notebooks.

When you teach with the TCI Approach, your lessons begin with a Preview assignment—a short, engaging task that foreshadows upcoming content. Some Previews challenge students to predict what a lesson will be about; others draw a parallel between key social studies concepts and students' lives. The goal is to spark interest, activate prior knowledge, tap a wide range of intelligences, and prepare students to tackle new concepts.

At the lower-elementary levels, Preview activities might involve Big Books, games, songs, group brainstorming, or interaction between pairs. As students begin to develop writing skills, they often complete written Preview assignments in their Interactive Student Notebooks. The Interactive Student Notebook is a powerful classroom tool for organizing student learning, which you will learn more about in other sections of this book. Turning to the Preview assignment in their notebook gets students thinking about the work to come and sets them up for success with the rest of the lesson.

Examples of Preview Assignments

There is no single formula for a good Preview assignment. The TCI Approach encourages a wide variety of paths into a lesson. Following is a variety of Preview activities from *Social Studies Alive!*

Identifying Problems and Solutions
One lower-elementary lesson turns the spotlight on four community problem solvers from America's past, teaching children that one person can make a difference in a community. As a Preview activity for this lesson, children identify a problem they have noticed in the classroom or at school, such as a messy reading area or litter on the playground, and suggest ways to fix the problem. This helps them appreciate, later in the lesson, the role other people have played in improving life in their communities.

After identifying and trying to solve problems in their own school, students can better appreciate urban problem solvers from the past, such as the man who invented the traffic light.

Brainstorming Ways of Being Good Helpers Another lower-elementary lesson leads children to discover the contributions they can make at school by helping others, respecting school property, being positive, and solving problems. The Preview activity for this lesson asks children to brainstorm ways they help at home, such as taking out the trash and feeding pets. They also practice making good choices about helping at home. This prepares the children to explore similar ways they can be good helpers at school.

The Geography Song

Every community big or small
Has its own geography.
With many different features,
I know what they're called.
Listen... I can name them all.
Mountains are the tallest land
the Earth has seen.
Valleys are low places in between.
Deserts are hot, dry places.
Some have sand.
A plain is a large, flat piece of
land.

Singing About Geographic Features In this lower-elementary lesson, students learn that communities have different geographic features and that physical maps show these features. As a Preview assignment, students listen to "The Geography Song," which mentions such key geographic features as mountains, valleys, deserts, and plains. After students have sung the song and seen pictures of each feature, they annotate the lyrics in their notebooks with a drawing of each feature.

Categorizing Six Communities Allowing students to discover key social studies concepts before they read about them is a powerful way to begin a lesson. For example, a lower-elementary lesson in which students compare rural, urban, and suburban communities begins with a Preview that is a categorization game. Students are shown six photographs of communities and asked to match images of similar communities. Students then suggest adjectives to describe each type of community, as preparation for the upcoming lesson.

Experiencing How Rules Help Us In a lower-elementary lesson, students learn why schools have rules. The teacher begins the Preview activity by telling students they will play a game in which there are two teams, each team gets a ball, and the fastest team wins. The teacher is evasive when children ask for clarification. As students play the "game," some are excited and energetic; others are concerned and confused. Afterward, the teacher asks students how they felt as they played and how the game could be improved. The teacher incorporates their suggestions into a second game with explicit rules and then debriefs the experience by asking, *How did you feel this time? Do you think it is important to have rules at school? Why?* This activity gives students the "mental framework" they need to better understand the lesson about why schools have rules.

In this Preview activity, students match and analyze photographs—such as these two images of urban communities—before reading about the different types of communities.

Talking About Travel Brochures In an upper-elementary lesson, students learn about the geography of communities around the country. The Preview activity introduces a travel brochure for an Alaskan city. In a group discussion, students identify key parts of the brochure and their purpose. This gives them the background they need for the main lesson activity in which they create their own travel brochures, highlighting the geographic features of a community they have explored.

Students view an illustration that depicts several public services as they listen to and identify sounds related to each of the public services.

Listening to the Sounds of Services in My Community One lower-elementary lesson, in which students learn about public services, begins with a musical Preview activity. Students are shown an illustration depicting various community services as they listen to a recording of related sounds such as a siren (police), a bus (public transportation), and children playing (child care services). After students identify all the sounds, the teacher asks what they think they will learn in the upcoming chapter. The visual and auditory experience provides a solid basis for the prediction and contributes to students' comprehension of the reading and lesson that follow.

Using a Graph An upper-elementary lesson explores how Midwestern farming practices have changed from 1800 to modern times. As a Preview activity, students graph data on the average number of people a farmer could feed in 1870, 1920, 1950, 1960, and 1970. The graph shows that, as the years have gone by, fewer farmers have been able to feed more people. Students hypothesize why this might be and what changes in farming have enabled this to happen—questions they will explore in the coming activities.

Connecting to the Idea of Scarcity In an upper-elementary lesson, students explore the history of how people have shared and tamed the water of the Colorado River. To introduce the idea of a limited resource, students are asked to remember a time when there was a limited supply of something that everyone wanted (for example, perhaps there were 12 children at a birthday party but only 10 cupcakes). Students write two or three sentences describing what happened, draw self-portraits showing how they felt, and write one sentence describing why they felt that way. The teacher then asks, *What is the best way to share something that is in short supply?* This gives students the context they need to understand fully the lesson about the history of the Colorado River.

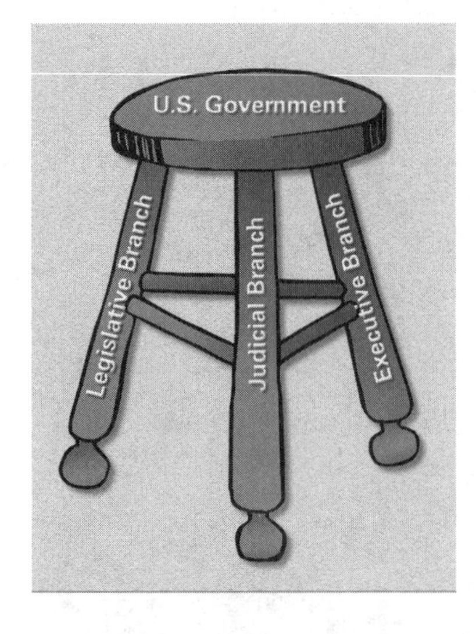

Discovering the Strength of a Three-Legged Stool Learning about the strength of a three-legged stool might seem an odd way to teach about the U.S. Constitution, but as a Preview activity it gives students an extremely memorable referent for understanding the complexities of our system of government. Students begin by trying to balance a book on the end of a pencil. After they struggle for a minute, they are asked to quickly form groups of three and to try balancing a book on the ends of three pencils. After they talk about which method was more successful, the teacher explains that—like a one-legged stool—the central government under the Articles of Confederation was weak, unstable, and ineffective. Students are told they will now read about how the delegates at the Constitutional Convention redesigned the government to create three strong branches (legs) to better meet the needs of the growing nation.

Understanding What a Dilemma Is In a Preview for another upper-elementary lesson, students learn that a dilemma is a situation requiring a choice between evenly balanced and usually unattractive options—for example, wearing boots you don't like, or getting your feet wet. In their notebooks, students write about a dilemma they have faced and how they responded to it. This prepares them for a lesson on the slave trade in which they learn about the difficult dilemmas faced by West Africans as European slave traders forced them from their homelands.

Using a Preview activity to encourage students to explore a dilemma they have faced will help them empathize with the dilemmas West Africans faced during the slave trade.

Multiple Intelligence Teaching Strategies

Walk into a classroom using the TCI Approach and *Social Studies Alive!* materials, and you will see one of these six powerful multiple intelligence teaching strategies in action: Visual Discovery, Social Studies Skill Builder, Experiential Exercise, Writing for Understanding, Response Groups, and Problem Solving Groupwork.

All six strategies are designed to involve students in their learning through active, hands-on experiences. Here are just a few examples: Students take on specific roles to design a neighborhood park; they perform a dragon dance as they learn about cultural celebrations; they explore visual and audio "artifacts" that represent different communities around the world; they play a buying-and-selling game that demonstrates how our economy works; they write a script for a "talking building" that tells about their state's history; they act as 19th-century settlers migrating into areas of the classroom that represent the western territories of the United States.

The following pages explain the basic steps to using these six strategies, all of which motivate students, capture their imaginations, and help you bring social studies alive.

To learn about the importance of water use issues in the West over time, students take on the roles of different people living near the Colorado River—including Native Americans, ranchers, city dwellers, power companies, and environmentalists. Is there enough water for everyone? What if we build dams? How does it feel to have to share the available water?

Multiple Intelligence Teaching Strategy

Visual Discovery

Steps at a Glance

1. Arrange your classroom so projected images will be large and clear.

Use a few powerful images to represent a lesson's key concepts.

Ask carefully sequenced questions that lead to discovery.

Challenge students to read about the image and apply what they learn.

5. Have students interact with the images to demonstrate what they have learned.

Even today's youngest elementary students are bombarded daily with media images. Constant exposure to television, videos, computer games, magazines, and advertisements has created a "visual generation." Many teachers are beginning to notice, however, that while students certainly "consume" many images daily, they don't always understand what they are seeing. In fact, far from being visually literate, many of our students have become so numbed by the sheer quantity and rapidity of media images that they have been left visually illiterate.

Visual Discovery activities turn the passive viewing of images into a dynamic, participatory experience. Students view, touch, interpret, and bring to life compelling images as they discover key social studies concepts. The strategy sharpens visual literacy skills, encourages students to construct their own knowledge through higher-level thinking, develops deductive reasoning, and taps visual, intrapersonal, and body-kinesthetic intelligences. It equips students to continue to "read" and analyze images even as they develop their reading skills. Best of all, this strategy is great fun and levels the cognitive playing field by allowing your nonlinguistic learners a chance to shine.

Arrange your classroom so projected images will be large and clear.

Careful attention to your classroom's geography is essential for a successful Visual Discovery activity. Most classroom arrangements actually inhibit interaction; students often sit in long rows or at tables far from the front of the classroom. A clutter of desks, tables, and file cabinets can make it difficult for students to see and touch projected images. To set up your classroom successfully, follow these steps:

1. **Identify the best wall on which to project images.** The wall should be in an area of the room that you can make fairly dark. Project a sample transparency on the wall, and make the image as large as possible. The larger you project an image, the more interaction and excitement you will generate.

2. **Create a screen.** If buying a large screen is cost prohibitive, you can easily create your own. Simply tape butcher paper to the wall to create a screen at least 8 feet tall by 8 feet wide. Or tape together two 4-foot-by-8-foot, 1-inch-thick insulating foam boards, found in many building-supply stores. If you want a screen that can roll up, you can purchase a large window shade.

3. **Design a floor plan of exactly where you want students to sit.** You may need to try a few configurations before deciding exactly how you want your students and their desks arranged. Lower-elementary teachers usually have students sit on the carpet in front of the image (see Map 1). They move all other furniture out of the way of the image; in the darkened room, students can then quickly and safely get up to "touch" the image. Upper-elementary teachers have students form their desks or tables into a crescent shape (see Map 2) or a parliamentary configuration (see Map 3).

4. **The first time you arrange your classroom for a Visual Discovery activity should be when students are not in class and you can try out various configurations.** Once you have found an arrangement that works, prepare a transparency to show your students exactly how to set up the room. If they need to move desks or tables, consider putting small marks or bits of tape on the floor to indicate where they are to position the furniture.

5. **Make sure you can darken the room enough for the transparency to really "pop."** Too much light will make the image difficult to see and give students trouble locating fine details. If necessary, cover the windows with dark paper. Or, if your room becomes pitch dark when you turn off the lights, use table lamps to create low-level lighting.

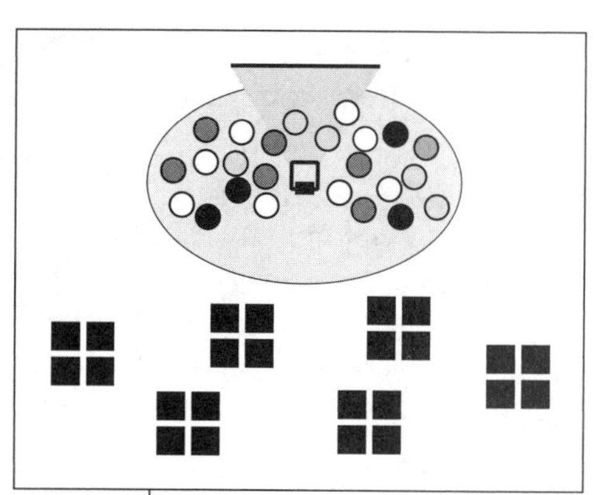

Map 1: Seating arrangement for lower-elementary classroom

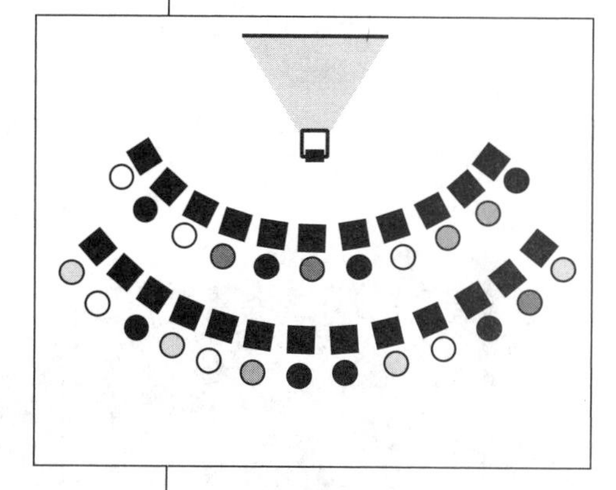

Map 2: Seating arrangement for upper-elementary classroom

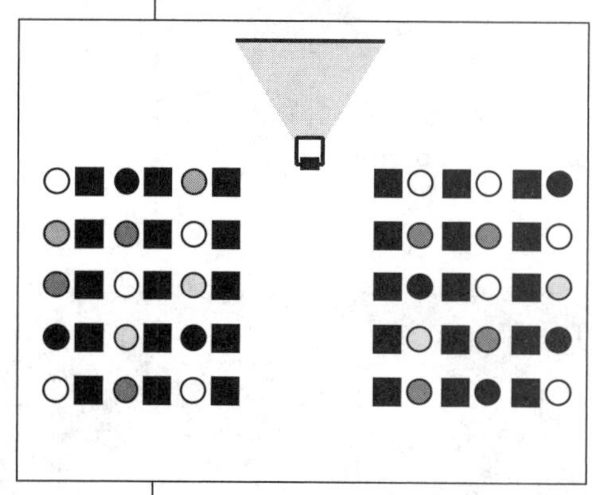

Map 3: Seating arrangement for upper-elementary classroom

"Since I've been using the Visual Discovery strategy, my students automatically want to dissect any image, on the overhead or in a textbook. I've seen them sit quietly, looking at a picture much longer than before, because they are 'reading' all the details. It has become a habit for the kids."

STEP 2

Use a few powerful images to represent a lesson's key concepts.

The key to a successful Visual Discovery activity is using a few powerful images that represent the key concepts of the lesson. The right image will stay in your students' minds for months, or even years, and will serve as a powerful visual referent to help them recall key social studies concepts.

Selecting only a few strong images enables you to spend quality time helping students "read" each image and develop their visual literacy skills. Since images won't be shown as fast-paced videos or computer animations, it is essential that each tells a rich story. Here are characteristics of images that will grab your students' attention and allow you to "work" a single image for up to 5 minutes with lower-elementary students and 10 minutes with upper-elementary students:

Use images that clearly convey the key concepts you are trying to teach. If you are trying to teach the differences among rural, urban, and suburban communities, for example, use only one or two images of each type of community. Each image you choose should be richly detailed. For example, a photo of a suburban community should include homes, cars, quiet streets, and a few people.

This photograph of a suburban community is rich in visual details.

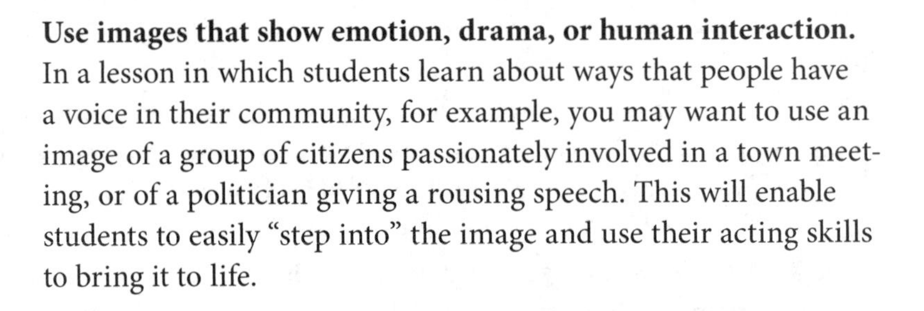

Use images that show emotion, drama, or human interaction. In a lesson in which students learn about ways that people have a voice in their community, for example, you may want to use an image of a group of citizens passionately involved in a town meeting, or of a politician giving a rousing speech. This will enable students to easily "step into" the image and use their acting skills to bring it to life.

Use images with abundant details that are connected to the reading. A wonderful way to improve students' reading comprehension is to ask them questions about a projected image, have them read a related passage, and then ask them to connect details from their reading to the image. For example, you might project a photograph of an Inuit family sitting in front of their shelter made of stitched-together animal skins. After students have examined the photo, give them a reading focused on how the Inuit adapted to their environment. They should then be able to use their newfound knowledge to point out several examples in the photograph of how the Inuit adapted to their Arctic environment.

Students can easily act out this image of a town meeting.

Use a variety of images. Use different sorts of images—photographs, illustrations, paintings, maps, cartoons—to captivate student interest. Images with bold colors, simple messages, or rich details work best.

Ask carefully sequenced questions that lead to discovery.

For each image you project, ask a series of questions that spiral from the basic to the critical-thinking level. The projected transparency is the primary source around which you will ask these questions. Students often want to analyze images with interpretive statements without carefully inspecting all the visual details. Move to the next level of questioning only when most of your students can "see" the answers to your questions. In this way, you will give them the building blocks they need to understand the most important social studies concepts related to each image. To keep engagement high, show a new image every 5 to 15 minutes or until you feel students have a satisfactory understanding of the concepts.

This sequence of questions will allow all students to discover a wealth of information about this photograph:

- What do you see in this image?
- Describe the structure you see and what is hanging from it.
- What are the people doing?
- What are they wearing?
- What can you tell about the environment in which these people live?
- How have these people used the natural resources in their environment to survive?

Here are some hints to help you get the most from the visual-inquiry process:

The first question to ask is always this: *What do you see in this image?* Don't move to the next question until students can point out many details in the image. You might ask several students to stand around the image and actually "touch" the details they see. This will give your students the foundation they need to answer the higher-level questions you will soon ask.

To increase interaction among all students, ask a question and allow pairs of students up to a minute to discuss it. Then have them share their ideas with the class.

Use a "detective analogy" to create spiral questions that will help your students better analyze and interpret visuals. Ask students to think of an image as a "scene from a time or place" that they, as detectives, need to investigate. Level 1 questions explain the details—what a detective would call evidence—that students could actually touch if they were somehow able to step into the scene. Level 2 questions challenge students to formulate ideas or make inferences based on the existing evidence. Level 3 questions encourage them to consider the scene as a whole and make hypotheses about what is happening and why, much as a detective surmises motive for an event.

Teach your students basic visual literacy skills they can use for each new image you display. Lower-elementary students can be taught to point to the top, bottom, right, and left of an image. Upper-elementary students should be able to point out details in each quadrant (upper right, lower left; or northeast, southwest to reinforce geography skills) and distinguish between the background and foreground.

Use "Magic Paper"

To focus students' attention on a specific part of a projected image, hold a large, stiff piece of white paper about 20 inches in front of it. A detail from the image will appear to be magnified on the paper.

Challenge students to read about the image and apply what they learn.

Now that you have asked carefully crafted spiral questions about an image and students have used their visual literacy skills to analyze that image, you are ready to have them read about the image. They will then apply what they have read to further analyze the image. Elementary teachers are finding that this simple yet powerful technique is helping their students become skilled and inspired readers. Here is an example of this approach in action:

After using their visual-literacy skills to discover how the Inuit adapted to their environment, students are eager to read in more detail about how the Inuit lived.

1. **Students spend ten minutes analyzing the image of the Inuit family at their camp in northern Alaska.** The teacher has helped students reach these conclusions about the Inuit: *The Inuit live in the Arctic. It is a cold, harsh environment. They have used some type of animal furs to create clothing and shelter. The Inuit live together in small family groups. They have dogs.* Having discovered a lot about the Inuit on their own, students are eager to continue the learning process.

2. **Students are now challenged to complete a six-paragraph reading on the Inuit and look for "ten details" that also are in the photograph.** They enthusiastically open their books and pour over the text, searching for more information, and discover a wealth of details: *The Inuit sewed together walrus, seal, and polar bear skins to make clothing, blankets, and tents. They burned animal fat for fuel. They filled sealskins with air. When attached to a harpoon that was thrown into the side of a whale, the inflated skins would float behind the whale and eventually tire it out.*

3. **After completing their reading, students have many more details about Inuit adaptations to help them interpret the photograph.** Eyes shine, hands wave, and the class buzzes with excitement as students share their new knowledge of Inuit adaptations. They can be heard exclaiming, "I didn't notice the rocks holding down the tent against the Arctic winds!" and "Look at the two blown-up sealskins hanging from the poles. They're used as floats!"

4. **When students are now asked to share ten details from their reading *not shown* in the photograph, they are just as informed and excited.** They mention such Inuit adaptations as snow goggles, igloos, knives, and harpoons.

Using images to motivate and set the context for reading will help you increase your students' literacy. Your students, especially those lacking strong linguistic skills, will experience success interpreting visuals and be more motivated to read. They will also have a better context to understand what they read. This will translate into greater effort and patience; as they read they will be working hard to discover more details than ever before. Ultimately, this approach helps individual students and the entire class become better critical thinkers.

Have students interact with the images to demonstrate what they have learned.

How do you assess what students have learned during a Visual Discovery activity? This is where the fun really begins. After all your hard work helping students to interpret each image, you get to sit back and watch them "step into" the images and bring them to life. Your students will now use their visual, body-kinesthetic, intrapersonal, interpersonal, and logical intelligences to demonstrate what they've learned. Here are three ways you can kindle their imagination and motivate them to show you what they have learned:

Talking Statues In a lesson designed to teach lower-elementary students the typical duties of a school teacher, principal, secretary, and custodian, students are asked to "step into" a projected image of one of these school workers and create a "talking statue." For example, for the image of the principal, students form three groups. The first group is encouraged to think about something a principal does to help students; the second, something a principal does to help families; and the third, something a principal does to help teachers. The teacher then "interviews" each group, asking such questions as, *Who are you? What are you doing? How do you help at your school?*

These students are bringing to life what they have learned about what a principal does to help students, families, and teachers.

Simulated Trips In another lesson, students act as space shuttle astronauts returning to Earth and seeing various geographic features—first, hemispheres, continents, oceans, and then a country, state, and city—coming into focus as they near their landing site. Students begin by lying on the floor in two rows in front of the screen, bending their legs with their feet on the floor. As they look out the space shuttle's window (the screen), they listen to a CD playing the sounds of rockets and NASA's communications with them. As they see closer and closer images of Earth through their shuttle window, they guess in which hemisphere, country, state, and city they will be landing. They identify each feature on individual maps as they near their target.

Cue Cards and Props In a lesson about how agriculture in the Midwest changed from 1800 to today, students act out various images of farm life through the two centuries. For each act-it-out, they are given cue cards and props to help them put on more detailed performances. For example, to help them bring to life an image of a woman washing clothes on a midwestern farm in 1900, students are given a picture of a washboard to use as a prop and a cue card with these questions: *What are you doing? How do you get the clothes dry? What do you dislike about the job? How often do you have to do this job?* The cue card also contains these hints: *Discuss how the performer can make the character come alive. Decide how the character can pantomime the job. Collect simple props to use during the act-it-out.*

"Children love the magic of make-believe. As their teacher, I enter this exciting child's world and endear myself to them when we 'act it out.' All my students love Visual Discovery lessons. The only problem is responding to the plea, ' Do it again! Oh please, may we do it again?' "

Multiple Intelligence Teaching Strategy

Social Studies Skill Builder

Steps at a Glance

1 Use Social Studies Skill Builders to engage and inspire your students.

2 Teach the skill through modeling and guided practice.

3 Prepare students to work in pairs.

4 Set clear expectations, allow students to practice the skill repeatedly, and give immediate feedback.

5 Debrief the lesson to help students make connections to key social studies concepts.

Social studies skills—such as reading maps, categorizing information, analyzing artifacts and primary resources, comparing and contrasting ideas, reading for detail, summarizing the main idea in writing, and interpreting historical documents—are vital to a student's success in middle and high school. Sadly, by the time your students reach the secondary level, their teachers may be so hard-pressed to cover content that they rarely have time to teach skills. You can prepare your students for success by giving them a strong foundation in the skills they will need to master more difficult content in middle and high school. Because they are fun, engaging, and fast-paced, Social Studies Skill Builders will allow you to begin teaching these skills as soon as students enter kindergarten.

In this strategy, students work in pairs to complete skill-oriented tasks. You begin each activity by quickly modeling the skill and then challenging students to practice that skill again and again. As students work, you give them immediate feedback. The activity ends with a debriefing session that allows students to use their new skill to make connections to key social studies concepts.

Use Social Studies Skill Builders to engage and inspire your students.

Teaching the skills elementary students will need to be successful in social studies courses during their secondary school careers may seem daunting. Using Social Studies Skill Builders, you can turn this formidable challenge into fun, interactive lessons that both you and your students will enjoy. The first step is to appreciate these unique features of Social Studies Skill Builders:

Students sit in pairs to solve skill-oriented problems. Working with just one partner gives each student more opportunity to talk and be involved than when working in a group.

Each task challenges students to use multiple intelligences. For example, in a lesson about how five racial and ethnic groups—Native Americans, Latinos, European Americans, African Americans, and Asian Americans—came to America and contributed to the country's growth and development, students read about each group, draw images and symbols to represent each group's experience, create a collage of the images, and write a verse that relates to each group.

Each skill is introduced quickly, and students are challenged to practice it repeatedly. Active involvement is the key to success.

Students are told exactly how their mastery of the skill will be assessed. For example, during an activity in which students analyze artifacts related to public services—such as drawings of a fire hose, fire hydrant, ax, and fire helmet to represent fire fighting—students must carefully write about what they think each artifact is, what it is used for, who would use it, and what public service it is related to. Students are given immediate feedback on each artifact they analyze. This pushes them to work quickly and creates a game-like atmosphere.

Each skill is taught at a developmentally appropriate level. If a skill is introduced thoughtfully, elementary students can master fairly complex topics sooner than you might expect. For example, lower-elementary students can learn how to understand perspective in a map if you begin by identifying objects in the classroom and then tell a story about a mouse that crawls to the top of the shelves and looks down upon the classroom. Using the idea of the mouse's perspective, students are then challenged to interpret a map of the classroom. In this way, young students learn basic map skills, which they will use for the rest of their lives.

In this Social Studies Skill Builder, lower-elementary students practice the social skills of talking and listening.

"Students enjoy Social Studies Skill Builders because they get to work with someone and the activities are fast-paced—they don't realize how much work they are actually doing. And I really appreciate that these are gradable activities without take-home paperwork for me."

STEP 2 Teach the skill through modeling and guided practice.

Introduce each Social Studies Skill Builder by quickly modeling and leading your students through guided practice of the skill. Teaching the skill consists of carefully explaining, and having students practice, each step before turning them loose to work on their own. Here are steps you could take to prepare students for a Social Studies Skill Builder in which they "excavate a sunken ship" to learn about the motives of 15th- and 16th-century European explorers:

In this upper-elementary Social Studies Skill Builder, students work in teams to learn about the motives of European explorers.

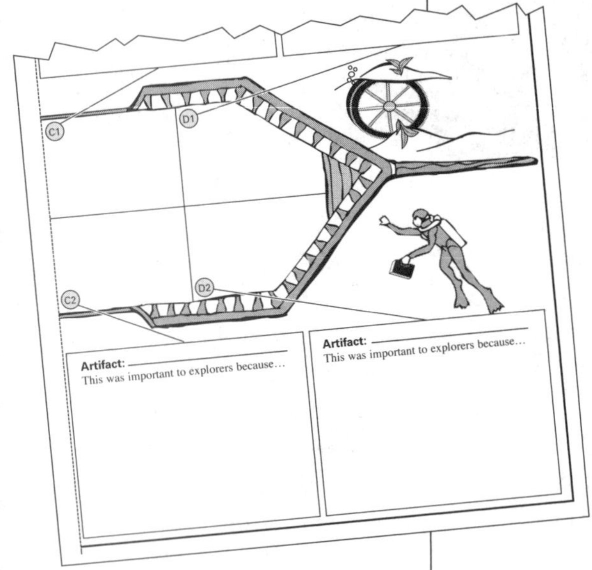

1. **Tell students that they will work in pairs and act as underwater archaeologists excavating a sunken ship.** Explain that they will soon learn how to retrieve artifacts (pictures) from a sunken ship's hull (outlined in tape on the floor), determine what they are, and draw conclusions regarding European exploration.

2. **Ask each pair to share the respective roles of diver and research scientist for the first artifact they bring to the ocean's surface.** They will switch roles for each new artifact.

3. **Show the divers how to simulate swimming motions and to enter the hull of the wrecked ship to retrieve an artifact.** Play underwater sound effects while students practice this.

4. **Show all students how to use geography skills to note on their underwater maps the grid section—such as D2—from which the artifact was taken.** Be sure everyone masters the skill.

5. **Show the divers how to bring the artifacts to a research station (desk) on "land."**

6. **Model for all students how to examine an artifact carefully, sketch it quickly, and find information in the text that sheds light on what the artifact is and what it was used for.**

7. **Explain that once pairs have identified and read about the artifact, they must finish this sentence: *This was important to explorers because....*** Model one or two sentences for them.

8. Demonstrate how you will review pairs' work. Show them how to stand patiently in line until you are ready to correct their assignments. Or become the "senior research scientist," making the rounds to the research stations to check for accuracy and to approve another dive. Explain that if an answer is wrong, pairs may have a chance to correct it to receive full credit.

9. Tell students that when their work has been corrected, they will dive back into the ship to return the artifact and choose another one to study. Have them study as many artifacts as possible in the allotted time.

"Be prepared to hear, 'May we PLEASE do this again tomorrow? It was so much fun!'"

Prepare students to work in pairs.

After you have modeled the skill, it's time to place students in pairs. Because they will be discussing skill-oriented questions that have discrete answers, working in pairs is ideal. Students will have more opportunity for interaction and won't get off track as easily as they might in a larger group. Here are some tips for preparing students to work in pairs:

Arrange students in mixed-ability pairs. Since these skill tasks require the use of multiple intelligences, it makes sense to pair students with complementary abilities. This will help ensure that each partner has something of value to contribute, and that interaction is more equitable. For an activity that requires linguistic and visual skills, for example, try to put a strong linguistic student with one who excels visually. This process may take a half hour, but it is time well spent as it will result in students working together much more harmoniously.

"Some students have such strength in a skill needed for the task that I make them 'experts' available to other pairs for consultation. The variety of skills needed for Social Studies Skill Builders gives me the opportunity to use many different experts, and students' self-esteem is very positively affected."

Before class, prepare a transparency showing where students will sit. Create a map showing the arrangement of desks or tables in your classroom or, for younger students, the location of the rug or community area. To limit distractions, space desks evenly around the classroom. Use an erasable marker to write students' names next to the desks at which you want them to work. This will help students move efficiently into pairs and will reinforce geography skills, especially if you add a compass rose to your map. Use the transparency as a template for your next Social Studies Skill Builder.

Instruct students to sit side by side on the rug, at tables, or with their desks touching. Project the map for students to use as a guide in forming pairs. Tell them they are not officially a team until they are sitting on the rug or at a table with their shoulders touching, or until the right edge of one desk is touching the left edge of the other and both students are facing forward.

Encourage students to greet each other. Once students have found their partners and are sitting correctly, tell them to introduce themselves and shake hands. Model this behavior with one of your students. Smile and have fun while you do this. This will ease tension and help pairs work together more effectively.

Conduct a quick team-builder to warm up students for working together. This might be as simple as having students look directly into their partners' eyes as they, with conviction and spirit, say, "Buddy, if you need a helping hand, you can count on me!" and give each other a high-five. You might also ask them to discuss a question relating to the skill being taught. For example, before an activity on public services, you might ask partners to share which of four public service jobs—teacher, firefighter, judge, or police officer—they would most like to have and why.

A bit of silliness in the classroom will help students feel comfortable and work together effectively.

Making Your Job Easier

You might create cards folded to show three surfaces—colored red, yellow, and green—and have groups signal their current working condition by flipping their card. Green means "We're fine, making progress." Yellow means "We have a question, but we'll continue to try to solve our own problem." Red means "We have finished our task and need to be checked but will continue to read and research while waiting." This encourages students to make wise use of their time and to take responsibility for helping themselves learn.

Checking work as students proceed through the activity helps keep students on task.

Set clear expectations, allow students to practice the skill repeatedly, and give immediate feedback.

After you have quickly modeled the skill and placed students in mixed-ability pairs, clearly state what you expect from them so you can evaluate their work fairly. An easy and efficient way to do this is to create a transparency that tells students exactly what is expected of them. You may want to award points for each part of an assignment your students successfully complete.

Checking work and awarding points as students progress through the activity will motivate them to work quickly and conscientiously in a game-like atmosphere. It will also assure that students create high-quality products, as they know you'll be carefully scrutinizing each answer. And it will give you a break from grading papers at home.

The greatest challenge you will face when giving students immediate feedback is managing the constant, and possibly overwhelming, flow of students waiting to have their work checked. Here are some tips to help make sure you have no more than two or three pairs of students waiting for feedback:

- Familiarize yourself with the handout in advance so you can quickly check each student's work for key points.
- Have students put their fingers on the exact answer they want corrected. This will prevent your having to search the entire handout for the next answer to correct.
- Give pairs more than one artifact or question to work on at a time so they take longer to finish.
- Ask students who have accurately completed the activity to be responsible for correcting their peers' work.
- Circulate around the classroom to correct handouts rather than having students wait in line. Students might signal they are ready for your review by putting their pencils down, folding their arms, and smiling—not by yelling for your attention.

Debrief the lesson to help students make connections to key social studies concepts.

Most teachers find that there comes a point during each Social Studies Skill Builder when most students, but not all, have finished working. It may be more effective to debrief the activity at this point than to wait for everyone to finish. To ensure that all your students have been exposed to the same content, consider asking pairs to take turns reporting to the class what they discovered. A pair might interpret an artifact, explain a primary source, or answer a geography question for the entire class while the other students take notes to make the information their own.

Having students group themselves along a spectrum helps the entire class to think holistically about the various pieces of information they collected during the activity.

After all your students have been exposed to all the content, it is time to challenge them to think holistically about the fragmented bits of content they have learned. Think of a way for your students to consider, as a whole, all the artifacts, questions, or primary resources they analyzed during the Social Studies Skill Builder. Here are some activities used to wrap up Social Studies Skill Builders:

- **Write an acrostic including all the examples they analyzed.** After a lesson in which students learn about public services by connecting a series of artifacts to specific services, challenge them to write an acrostic using the word PUBLIC. For example, the P might introduce the line, "Police make sure people are safe."
- **Write song verses about various groups in American society.** After students have analyzed a series of readings about racial and ethnic groups in the United States, ask them to write several verses to the song "This Land Is Your Land" that identify each group's country of origin and highlight the group's contributions to American society.
- **Create a photo journal of key geographic landmarks.** After students have located a series of physical features on a U.S. map, have them create a "photo journal" of a trip across the states by drawing geographic landmarks (Appalachians, Great Plains, Colorado River) seen along the way.
- **Create a "human spectrum" evaluating the contributions of European explorers.** After students have studied how ten European explorers claimed, conquered, and controlled North America, have individual students hold up a placard of each explorer and stand along a spectrum from "Explorer with Most Impact on the United States Today" to "Explorer with Least Impact on the United States Today."
- **Identify the effects of local geographic features.** After students have learned how geography impacts human settlement around the United States, have them select a geography topic—such as weather, elevation, natural resources, or bodies of water—that affects them locally and make a drawing showing the effects of that topic on people's lives.

"Debriefing Social Studies Skill Builders gives me a chance to make sure all students understand the concepts. I've found that after they have worked in pairs, they have a lot of details and ideas to share with the class."

Multiple Intelligence Teaching Strategy

Experiential Exercise

Steps at a Glance

1 Use Experiential Exercises to help students truly grasp key social studies concepts.

2 Prepare your students for a safe, successful experience.

3 Make the experiences as authentic as possible.

4 Allow students to express their feelings immediately after the experience.

5 Ask carefully sequenced questions to help students make connections between their experience and key concepts.

With the many concepts students are introduced to during their elementary years, it is no wonder they rarely remember key social studies concepts when they enter middle school. Yet an awareness of basic economics, geography, history, and civics concepts is the foundation for success in middle and high school social studies classes. Experiential Exercises are one way to ensure that your students grasp and remember even the highest-level concepts.

Experiential Exercises tap into students' intrapersonal and body-kinesthetic intelligences, allowing students to "experience" key social studies concepts. These short, memorable experiences make abstract ideas accessible and meaningful. For example, to help students understand how globalization affects their community, you assign each student a country and give them cards representing each country's products. As they sit in a circle, students simulate international trade by rolling a ball of yarn across the circle, eventually forming a trade web that connects them all. To experience the concept of population density, students huddle in a small area of the classroom and consider how they might adapt to such cramped conditions. And to learn why we need rules in school, students are challenged to play a game without rules so that they appreciate the need for them. Students react to these encounters as if they were real life, gaining an appreciation of key social studies concepts that they will remember long after their elementary years.

Use Experiential Exercises to help students truly grasp key social studies concepts.

Experiential Exercises awaken students to the richness and importance of key social studies concepts. However, they should be used thoughtfully and selectively. As you prepare to teach Experiential Exercises, keep in mind the following ideas.

These students have taken on the role of buyers and sellers at a fruit market. This hands-on experience will allow them to truly internalize the economics concept of supply and demand.

Use them when you need to quickly capture a moment or feeling that is central to your students' appreciation of social studies. Some concepts are so fundamental to social studies that, unless students truly grasp them, little will be gained from your teaching. Supply and demand, for example, is a fundamental economics concept—yet it would hardly be effective to present elementary students with graphs showing supply-and-demand curves. Instead, you might use an Experiential Exercise in which students become fruit sellers and buyers, with simple props representing money and fruit. Tell buyers that their objective is to buy as much fruit as they can with $4. Tell sellers that their objective is to make as much money as possible. Afterward, ask questions designed to reveal the concept of supply and demand: *What strategies did buyers use to get the most fruit? What strategies did sellers use to make the most money? What happened to the price of fruit as the activity went on?*

Use them when your teaching objective centers on a topic that is best taught through body-kinesthetic or intrapersonal intelligence. Some social studies lessons are best absorbed through physical or emotional experience. To help your students learn how the American colonies defeated Britain in the Revolutionary War, for example, have them engage in a tug-of-war in which you change the rules to favor a seemingly weaker team, much as a number of factors ultimately helped the colonies win the war. Students will never forget how the smaller, colonial team started from behind but ultimately won because you made the "British army" run across the room to join the war and allowed "French allies" to come to the colonists' aid. They will literally have a "muscle memory" of why the Americans won.

Use them when you want to evoke an emotional response so that students empathetically react to social studies concepts they might otherwise find remote or unimportant. Experiential Exercises can be used to help students appreciate how people feel or react to various life situations. Lower-elementary students, for example, may not recognize that hurt feelings can result from poor social skills. Using an Experiential Exercise, you could have pairs of students silently share a crayon to draw a picture. This inevitably leads to frustration, as students who have not been taught cooperative skills struggle to complete the joint task. Debrief the activity, having students offer ways in which they can cooperate the next time they face a joint task. Then have them practice these behaviors—sharing, taking turns, listening, and talking—to draw another picture. This intrapersonal experience helps students discover the value of cooperation.

"Experiential Exercises help students form emotional and muscle-memory connections to the content. I've seen students, while working their way through a written assessment, glance over to where an Experiential Exercise took place the week before, accessing a mental image of what they did."

Consider Alternate Venues

If an Experiential Exercise requires a significant rearrangement of your classroom, consider setting it up in the school cafeteria or multipurpose room. This will give both you and your students a welcome break.

In this Experiential Exercise, students simulate the population density of various communities—such as the extremely high population density of New York City. To make this a safe experience, address safety issues before the activity begins.

Prepare your students for a safe, successful experience.

Experiential Exercises can be risky because you can't always control students' responses. The goal is to give students a memorable experience, so such strong emotions as frustration, joy, passion, and anger will sometimes surface. It is wise to take a few precautionary steps to ensure all goes well.

1. **Address safety concerns ahead of time.** If the Experiential Exercise requires students to play a game, such as a tug-of-war, or move around the classroom in unconventional ways, begin by clearly explaining how students are to move during the activity. Before a tug-of-war, for example, you might demonstrate the proper way to hold the rope.

2. **Arrange the classroom appropriately.** Many Experiential Exercises require unusual room arrangements. Set up the classroom before students arrive; if they must move tables or desks, time will be lost and students will be distracted. For example, an activity in which students take a "walking tour" of Williamsburg to learn about daily life in the colonial Virginia capital has students visit six stations. Each station represents a site at Williamsburg, such as the Governor's Palace and the Raleigh Tavern, and includes written and visual information to help students complete a task, such as playing a colonial game or singing a slave song. Having the stations in place before students enter the room saves instructional time, and the unusual classroom arrangement piques students' interest and readies them for the activity.

3. **Set clear behavioral and learning expectations.** While students find Experiential Exercises unusual and often fun, it is crucial to always set clear behavioral and learning expectations. You might begin by telling students: "What we are about to do might seem like a game, but I expect you to behave as if we were doing a regular activity. When it's over, I'll help you make connections between the game and the social studies concepts I want you to learn."

4. **Give students clear directions.** Most Experiential Exercises require students to participate in activities far different from those in conventional classrooms. Students need precise directions if they are to feel comfortable—in fact, an activity might fail if you give vague directions. Consider the activity in which students simulate a global trading network by rolling a ball of yarn. If you don't tell them precisely how to sit, pass the ball of yarn, and take turns, the yarn may end up wrapped around body parts or thrown through the air.

5. **Anticipate student reactions.** Take, as an example, an activity intended to teach lower-elementary students why schools have rules. Imagine how your students would react if you asked them to play a game with only these rules: there are two teams, each team gets a ball, and the fastest team wins. Your aggressive students will delight at this chance for anarchy, while students who need clear structure will be frustrated and uncomfortable. Experiential Exercises are designed to elicit strong emotional responses; being prepared to deal with them is the key to success with this strategy.

Make the experiences as authentic as possible.

Whether you are setting up a Civil War battlefield or simulating population density in New York, a key ingredient for successful Experiential Exercises is tapping into your "inner performer." You might think of these activities as interactive theater, and have fun acting, preparing your classroom, collecting props, and adding special effects. Here are several ways you can make Experiential Exercises so authentic that your students will never forget what they learned:

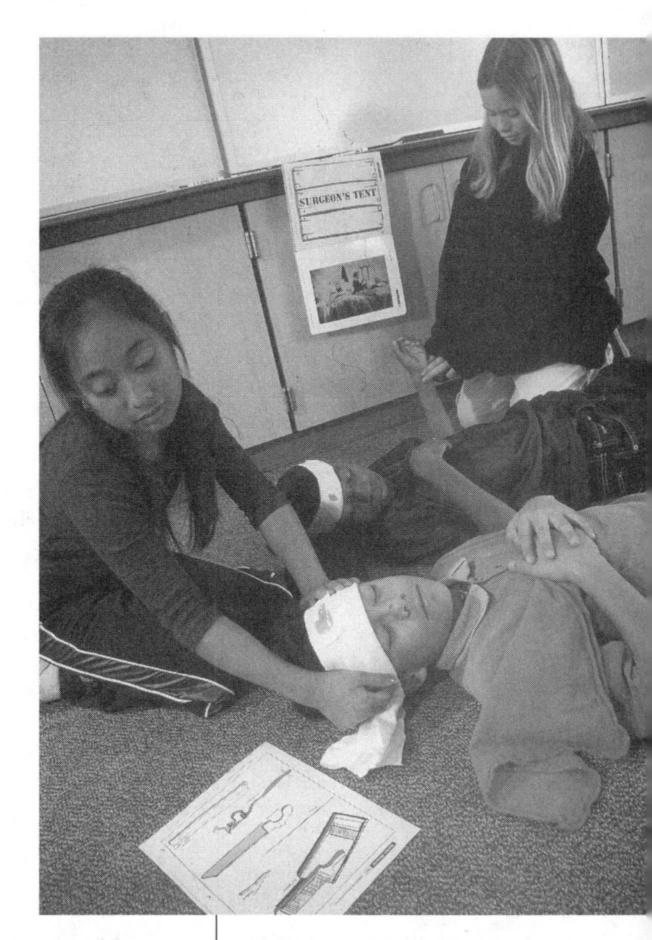

By re-creating a surgeon's tent during the Civil War, you help students experience the historical moment and make personal connections to concepts being studied.

Keep a straight face when appropriate. In some situations—such as asking students to share a crayon to draw a single picture (to learn the value of sharing and taking turns), or telling students they will be charged five cents per handout (to drive home the concept of taxation without representation)—you must maintain a serious demeanor. If you show amusement, students will know you are playing a trick on them, and the impact of the lesson will be lost.

Be dramatic when appropriate to heighten student interest. Before an economics lesson on the production and distribution of goods, for example, excitedly tell students, "Today you will all be allowed to go on a shopping spree!" Or, during a geography lesson on population density, exclaim with wonder and amazement at the vast number of people living in New York City.

Ham it up. You might be surprised at how contagious your enthusiasm can be. When your students are learning about how goods are transported to market, have them join you in making truck, boat, and airplane sounds. When they take a walking tour of colonial Williamsburg, make an exaggerated point of having them greet each other with this actual colonial salutation: "Greetings, friend. I am your most obedient and humble servant. I am heartily glad to see you." Students will revel in your example, resulting in a more authentic experience for all.

Use simple props and costumes. Most classrooms are filled with potential props. Desks can become mountains during a geography lesson; butcher paper can turn into transportation routes during an economics lesson; pieces of cloth can become colonial costumes, national flags, or blankets aboard an immigrant ship during a history lesson. Some teachers even ask their students to bring in props from home, such as clothing and sports equipment. Props add both authenticity and a sense of playfulness that helps center students' attention.

Use music and sound effects. Students who have strong musical intelligence will appreciate any attempt you make to reinforce social studies concepts through music and other sounds. You might have students join in a call-and-response song to dramatize colonial slave life, or listen to the sounds of a rushing river as they explore the history of how people have shared and tamed the water of the Colorado River. "Music memory" will help students remember key social studies concepts long after you turn off the CD player or stop singing.

"Experience Exercises are unforgettable. When former students return for a visit, the first thing they ask is, 'Are you still doing the tug-of-war?' or 'Do you still take the class to Williamsburg and Gettysburg?' And then they say, 'I really miss your history class.'"

Allow students to express their feelings immediately after the experience.

Experiential Exercises are designed to let students experience strong emotions connected to key social studies concepts so that they will long remember those concepts. Before you can make connections between the activity and the concept you are teaching, however, allow students to focus on the affect of their experience. Prompt them with this single question: "What feelings did you experience during this activity?" This question serves three purposes:

Students are encouraged to identify and articulate their feelings. Some students, particularly those with weaker intrapersonal intelligence, have difficulty describing their feelings. Focusing the initial portion of the class discussion on the affect of an Experiential Exercise helps all students better understand how they reacted. A poster displaying faces with various emotions—such as surprise, bewilderment, excitement, and sadness—may help lower-elementary students articulate their feelings. And older students often find a poster listing "feeling words"—such as *worried, disappointed,* and *scared*—helpful when trying to express their emotions.

Students are able to share their feelings in the proper environment. In a cooperative, tolerant classroom (described in Part 2 of this book), students feel safe to talk freely and honestly about how they felt and reacted. If this is not done during class time, students' emotions may spill over into other classes or at home.

Students know that their reactions are okay. Letting students discuss their feelings without judgment sends them a strong message: it is okay to have and share powerful emotions. This validation will establish a framework for the rest of the debriefing.

As the conversation unfolds, ample opportunities will arise to weave your content objectives into the discussion.

When the teacher places restrictions on a class party they have been planning, students feel frustrated, even powerless. These feelings, when fully expressed, will help students relate to the experience of the American colonists prior to the Revolutionary War.

STEP 5

Ask carefully sequenced questions to help students make connections between their experience and key concepts.

Once students have discussed their feelings, it's time to connect the experience to key social studies concepts. Prepare a list of carefully sequenced questions that enable students to draw connections between their experience and key concepts. Spiral the questions, from basic to higher-order thinking skills, so students can use their experience to grasp the new concepts.

"When an inaccuracy arises in the discussion, I usually give the comment a moment to sink in. Other students will usually correct the mistake. This way, the learning remains student-centered."

The questions should be carefully crafted to help students discover concepts and reach conclusions on their own; answering the questions yourself would rob your students of this opportunity. Here is a series of questions you might ask lower-elementary students after they have created a global trading network, using a ball of yarn:

- How did you feel during this activity?
- What do you notice about the web of yarn we have formed?
- Does the web of yarn connect everyone equally? Why or why not?
- In what ways do you think this activity is similar to the way real countries trade with each other?
- In what ways do you think this activity is unlike the way real countries trade with each other?

In a lower-elementary Experiential Exercise, students play a game without rules to help them discover why rules are needed. The teacher then debriefs the activity by asking such questions as these:

- How did you feel playing this game?
- Was this a good game? Why or why not?
- How could this be a better game?

Notice that the last two questions ask students to compare how the experience was both like and unlike reality. As students begin to explore how Experiential Exercises compare to real life, they begin to see the differences in magnitude, scope, and seriousness between the classroom activity and reality. Failing to do this after an Experiential Exercise simulating Civil War battlefields, for example, would trivialize the experience of Civil War soldiers. And neglecting to do so after an activity on buying and selling in the marketplace would risk students' underestimating the complexities of the free-enterprise system.

Carefully sequenced questions will go a long way to helping you facilitate a rich class discussion. In addition, be prepared to ask many follow-up questions that continually direct students to explore connections to the key concepts and help them get back on track when necessary. Many students, especially at the lower-elementary level, have a tendency to quickly get off track during these discussions because they are bubbling with excitement after the activity. Your task is to prevent this from happening. A great way to do this is to praise and recognize students when they make connections between the activity and real life. The result will be a rich classroom discussion—and great moments of learning.

Multiple Intelligence Teaching Strategy

Writing for Understanding

Steps at a Glance

1. Use writing to help your students learn key social studies concepts.

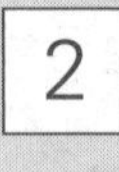
2. Give students rich experiences to write about.

3. Have students record their ideas, thoughts, and feelings in prewriting activities.

4. Provide students with authentic writing assignments.

5. Guide students through the writing process.

Have you ever given your students an engaging writing assignment, only to find they respond with poorly organized, incoherent prose? Take, for example, the fourth grade teacher who asked her students to write a letter to a friend describing places in the Northeast region of the United States. She believed that after reading their textbooks and filling out several worksheets, they would have plenty to write about. The letters, however, were uncreative and lacking in detail: "The Northeast is a part of the U.S. Lots of people live there. There is lots of land in the Northeast. The Northeast is a nice place to live." She felt that her students had learned little, if anything, about life in the Northeast. What had gone wrong?

In truth, this writing assignment and its predictable outcomes might be found in almost any upper-elementary classroom. A new approach to writing in the content area is vital. To write forcefully and in detail about social studies topics, students need interactive experiences about which to write. Writing for Understanding activities tap into students' multiple intelligences so that *all* learners have something memorable to write about. Before asking students to write such a letter, for example, you might take them on a simulated "train tour" of the Northeast in which they see the coast (a projected image), hear the call of a foghorn (a recording), and walk up several floors in the Empire State Building (stepping in place, 18 times for each floor). Let them record their thoughts, reactions, and feelings along the way, and then give them clear guidelines for writing the letter. Teachers are finding that such creative activities motivate students to write with style and meaning.

Use writing to help your students learn key social studies concepts.

Writing for Understanding activities will improve both your students' understanding of key social studies concepts and their writing ability. These activities will also help build a strong foundation in expository writing that will serve your students well throughout their lives. Here is why.

Writing during social studies activities supports students' writing fluency. Writing for Understanding activities help lower-elementary students move from scribbles to letters, to words, and, finally, to sentences. They give students concrete, meaningful experiences to write about. Upper-elementary students, who tend to be quite verbal, need to learn to communicate via the written word. They may begin with lists, categories, and sentence fragments. Ultimately, they discover how to "chunk" their learning and put what they've learned into cohesive paragraphs, stories, letters, dialogues, and essays.

Writing challenges students to clarify, organize, and express what they have learned. When students are asked to verbalize their understanding of a key social studies concept, they often respond with vague, unorganized thoughts. Requiring them to put their thoughts in writing challenges them to form explicit, detailed, and tangible ideas.

Writing enables students to reach a deeper understanding as they draw on prior learning for supporting detail. Too often students make generalizations or express opinions without supporting details or facts. Having students write about social studies is an excellent way to teach them the necessity of supporting arguments with solid evidence and precise details.

Ownership of written products motivates students to excel. Students will invest more time and energy in learning social studies if they are challenged to write creatively. If you encourage your students to develop their individual voices, their writing will become a form of self-expression rather than just a regurgitation of what they read in their textbooks.

The writing process compels upper-elementary students to refine their ideas. The writing process—brainstorming, writing rough drafts, revising, and editing—requires focused thinking and precise expression. Whereas the spoken word is transitory, a written idea can be reviewed, revised, and embellished. The process of writing a polished, well-supported piece leads to greater understanding of a topic.

Writing for Understanding activities inspire even lower-elementary students to write about what they've learned.

Give students rich experiences to write about.

Whether simple sentences, paragraphs, essays, or stories, writing done in the conventional social studies classroom typically lacks detail, style, and creative expression. At best, most writing efforts tend to be simple recountings of key vocabulary words.

To write powerfully, students need a variety of memorable, interactive experiences on which to base their writing. These activities must tap into the multiple intelligences to give all learners, even those with weaker linguistic skills, something to say. As students participate in these activities—see powerful images, role-play, discuss compelling issues, or act out key social studies concepts—they develop ideas and form opinions before they begin writing. Here are three examples of "real life" experiences that give students something tangible to write about:

Who Provides Services in a Community? In this lower-elementary lesson, students learn about service occupations. After viewing and discussing images of various service jobs, pairs of students randomly select a picture card of a service occupation, such as a cook, and bring it to life in a pantomime, using simple props. Their classmates try to guess which occupation they are pantomiming. In the subsequent writing assignment, students create a stick puppet with, for example, a drawing of a cook on one side and a simple job description on the other: "I am a cook. I work in a restaurant. I use pots, pans, and a stove. I like my job because I make hungry people happy."

How Are We Alike Around the World? In this upper-elementary lesson, students learn how their lives compare to those of children in other countries. Six youngsters from afar "travel to the classroom" on placards. To learn about Emma from Hungary, for example, students visit a station with a photograph of Emma in her native dress, information about her home and school life, and pictures of two artifacts: a flute and a sewing kit. They also listen to a recording of Emma playing her flute. Students identify similarities and differences between Emma's life and theirs. They use their experiences to write a letter to one of the children they "visited."

Students are anxious to write a letter about the Southwest after touring key sites on a "big rig."

A Big Rig Tour of the Southwest In this upper-elementary lesson, students "tour" the U.S. Southwest. When students enter the classroom, chairs are set up in rows of three (to simulate the front seat of a big rig). Students are told they will visit nine sites (projected images) on their tour and will hear about each site from their guide (a recording that includes sounds of the Southwest such as galloping horses and a Texas folk song). At three sites, students participate in an activity. For example, at the Guthrie, Oklahoma, stop, they re-create the settlement of Oklahoma, discovering the fates of Native Americans, boomers, ranchers, railroad men, sooners, and land-run participants. Finally, they write a detailed, two-page letter describing what they observed and what they learned on their Southwest tour.

Have students record their ideas, thoughts, and feelings in prewriting activities.

Prewriting activities allow students to record their reactions, feelings, reflections, and ideas immediately after the interactive experiences they have had. Even the most reluctant writers can be coaxed into crafting original, meaningful pieces if you begin the process by having them record their initial reactions with fun and engaging prewriting activities—such as matrices, flowcharts, sensory figures, or other types of graphic organizers that relate to the experience. At the lower-elementary level, prewriting might be conducted as a whole-class activity. Here are some examples of prewriting:

Fun prewriting activities allow lower-elementary students to experience early success with writing assignments. In one lesson, a prewriting game helps students identify possible actions that a "good citizen" might take. From this, they go on to write their own simple books about things they will do to be good citizens themselves, such as "Pick up litter" or "Eat lunch with someone who is lonely."

"My Family Is Special" In a lower-elementary lesson which teaches that every family has unique qualities, students create a simple book about their own family by completing a sentence and drawing a picture on each page. For the Preview, which doubles as a prewriting activity, the teacher displays pictures of different families and asks students to brainstorm all the ways families differ. The teacher lists students' ideas on the board in such categories as *family members, homes,* and *activities.* After a short reading, students make similar lists in their Interactive Student Notebooks. These recordings help children when they prepare their own family books.

Structured Matrices In an upper-elementary lesson about the geography of communities around the country, students create travel brochures for the communities they read about. To get the most from their reading, students first complete a visual matrix for three communities: Roseburg, Oregon; Las Cruces, New Mexico; and Gloucester, Massachusetts. For each community, they draw a simple map and list features of the physical geography (mountains, coastal plains, deserts), natural resources (trees, water, minerals), and climate (snow, rain, drought). The completed matrix gives them a wealth of information for creating their travel brochures.

Annotated Maps In an upper-elementary lesson in which students take a "van and airplane tour" of the West region of the United States, students sit in groups of three, listen to a tour guide, and view nine images of places in the West. They record their thoughts and reactions to each site on an annotated map of the West. They later use their notes to write a letter about their excursions.

Talking Buildings In an upper-elementary lesson, students learn about their state's history by creating "talking buildings." As a class, they brainstorm familiar and famous buildings that played an important role in shaping their state's history. Then, in pairs, they research a building, create a three-dimensional model, write a script that tells about one era in the state's history from the perspective of the building, place the building on a timeline, and, finally, bring the building to life to tell the story of their state's history.

Get It While It's Fresh

Ask students to begin writing during or immediately after an Experiential Exercise or other multiple-intelligence task. When they write in the midst of a classroom experience, their writing takes on the emotions of the moment and will be filled with rich detail.

STEP 4

Provide students with authentic writing assignments.

Authentic writing assignments—journals, poetry, stories, letters, and the like—motivate students to write with style and meaning. While traditional assignments, such as paragraphs and essays, are appropriate for some social studies topics, giving your students a wider variety of writing activities promotes experimentation and makes writing more exciting and novel. When a writing assignment is compelling enough for students to care about, inspired writing almost always follows. Here are five examples of authentic writing assignments that challenge students to write creatively and in detail about key social studies concepts:

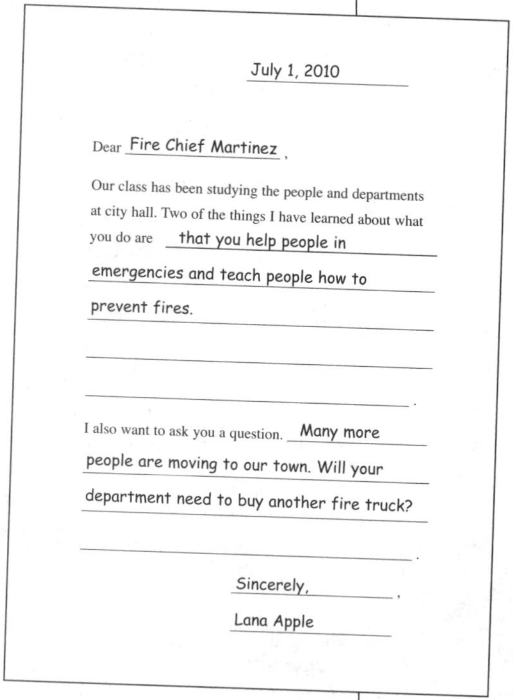

July 1, 2010

Dear Fire Chief Martinez,

Our class has been studying the people and departments at city hall. Two of the things I have learned about what you do are that you help people in emergencies and teach people how to prevent fires.

I also want to ask you a question. Many more people are moving to our town. Will your department need to buy another fire truck?

Sincerely,

Lana Apple

A civic letter

Civic Letters Nothing motivates great writing more than a true purpose. While they are learning about local government, encourage your lower-elementary students to write a letter to someone who works in the local government. The letter should address a problem or an opportunity the students think the government should attend to.

Script Reviews Upper-elementary students with a critical eye will love this assignment. After studying about Native American lifestyles in the Northwest during the 1700s, tell your students they are to critique a movie script in which Native Americans are shown wearing feathered headdresses, hunting buffalo, and living in teepees. Ask them to write a letter to the director that explains why this portrayal is inaccurate and suggests a more authentic way to portray Native American culture.

Journal Entries Most upper-elementary students relish the opportunity to write in a diary. After a make-believe tour in "crop dusters" through the Midwest region of the United States (accomplished with a few transparencies and a recording of a tour guide), students are challenged to write journal entries describing what they saw, heard, smelled, and felt along the trip.

A metaphorical story

Historical Plaques Creating different types of signs—such as historical plaques, museum labels, or road markers—will hold special appeal for your students with strong visual-spatial intelligence. For example, after they have studied the reasons the American colonies won the Revolutionary War, ask students to create a historical marker that commemorates the factors that allowed the Americans to win. The marker should include a summary of at least four factors that led to victory, each illustrated with a drawing.

Metaphorical Stories Students love to write stories based on metaphors. For example, while studying about the Civil War, challenge upper-elementary students to write about a feuding brother and sister. The illustrated story should show how the siblings' drama represents the tensions between the North and South that led to the Civil War.

Guide students through the writing process.

Once students have completed a prewriting activity and gathered several rough ideas and details, they are ready to focus on the rest of the writing process: following precise guidelines, writing a first draft, receiving peer feedback, revising the piece, and, finally, writing their final drafts. (The following process may be of greater concern to upper-elementary teachers, though many lower-elementary teachers use a very similar process.) Here are the next steps:

Peer-editing raises all students' awareness of spelling, grammar, and other aspects of their own writing.

1. **Give clear expectations and precise guidelines for writing assignments.** Confusion is a major obstacle to coherent writing. Give your students a handout that clearly states guidelines and deadlines for all parts of the assignment. Nothing will be more useful in helping students translate their rough ideas into a coherent piece of writing than this vital step.

2. **Have students write a first draft.** Once students finish organizing their ideas, have them experiment with an organizational structure in a first draft. Stress that while this draft does not have to be polished, it must be well organized and complete. Quickly review their drafts and note your suggestions.

3. **Use peer-feedback groups.** Divide your students into mixed-ability groups of three or four. Before students move into groups, emphasize that feedback should be honest, constructive, and specific. Each student in a group should use a different-color pen or pencil. Students exchange their papers with someone else in the group. When a student receives another's paper, she writes her name in the upper-right corner, marks any problems (younger students may just check word usage and spelling; older students may be able to comment on content, focus, organization, word choice, vividness of details, clarity of supporting examples, and the writer's voice), and passes the paper to another group member. When the author gets his paper back, he will know who made which suggestions, enabling him to seek further clarification as he writes his final draft.

Guidelines for Writing a Letter to a Global Friend

Write a letter to one of the children you learned about in this chapter. Make sure your letter includes these things:

- A **date**
- A **greeting** (for example: Dear Kazuo,)
- A **first paragraph** that tells the reader two things that are the same about your life and the child's life
- A **second paragraph** that tells the reader two things that are different about your life and the child's life
- **Drawings** showing two artifacts from your life that you mention in the letter
- A **closing** (for example: Your new friend,)
- **Your signature** (your name)

Precise writing guidelines double as a simple, ready-made rubric for the basic requirements of an assignment.

4. **Require students to make revisions.** Students should use the feedback they received from you and their peers to revise their original drafts.

5. **Have students edit their final drafts.** Before they turn in their final drafts, require students to have their papers edited by someone else—a classmate, a parent, or another teacher—before turning them in. Tell students that if their editor finds many errors, they must rewrite the paper. Minor changes can be made directly on the final draft.

Multiple Intelligence Teaching Strategy

Response Groups

Steps at a Glance

1 Create and move students into Response Groups.

2 Give students resources that inspire critical thinking.

3 Ask provocative critical thinking questions.

4 Allow groups time to prepare their responses.

5 Facilitate a lively class discussion.

Imagine your students immersed in a lively discussion of what to do about a polluted lake. Students politely take turns, listen to each other, and share opinions. Teachers know that being able to share and understand different points of view is essential in social studies—history, geography, economics, and civics. A wonderful way to cultivate different points of view and inspire critical thinking is through rich class discussion. In many elementary classes, however, in-depth, lively content discussions are rare. Response Groups will help you create such discussions and give your students the skills they need for engaging in and enjoying social studies throughout their school careers.

Begin by putting your students into small, mixed-ability groups. Give the groups a thought-provoking question to discuss and resources to stimulate them—such as photographs, music, simple artifacts, or key information. Soon you'll be watching your students excitedly gathering ideas from one another. After a few minutes, invite a presenter from each group to share the group's ideas with the class. You'll be witness to an entirely new level of interaction as your students respectfully vie with each other to communicate their ideas.

Create and move students into Response Groups.

The first step for succeeding with Response Groups is to create mixed-ability teams of students that know how to sit together in the correct formation. Here are some quick tips that will get you and your students off to the right start.

1. **Carefully form groups before the activity begins.** Try to put students with a variety of abilities in each group. For example, if the activity will involve drawing and writing, make sure each group has members with strong artistic and linguistic skills. If the topic explores cultural or gender issues, reflect ethnic or gender diversity within the groups.

2. **Before they move into groups, remind your students of the rules for creating a cooperative, tolerant classroom environment:**
   - Treat everyone, including the teacher, with respect.
   - Use kind words and actions toward others.
   - Do everything you can to help yourself and others learn.

   (The process of establishing these rules is discussed in Part 2, "Creating a Cooperative, Tolerant Classroom.")

3. **Create a clever and efficient way for students to move into groups that are carefully arranged so that students can easily talk to one another.** If the activity will involve a displayed image, make sure everyone will be able to see it. You might use a transparency, small marks on the floor, a dry-erase board, or a flannel board to show students which group they are in and where the group will gather.

4. **Have students practice moving into Response Groups.** In lower-elementary classes, they will quickly move from their desks to sit with their groups on the floor with their knees touching. In upper-elementary classes, moving into groups may involve rearranging some furniture. You might conduct a "Desk Olympics" to teach students to move desks quickly and safely. (The Desk Olympics is explained in Part 2 of this book.) Also, consider asking three volunteers to model how to quickly get into a group. Challenge them to discover ways to move into a group without touching each other or making any sounds. They may come up with very useful suggestions—such as putting the desks around them in the correct formation before they move into their groups, gesturing politely to indicate who should go where, and being considerate (including bowing to each other!) as they race around the classroom to get into formation.

5. **Wait to begin the activity until all groups are arranged precisely.** This sends a clear message: exact group configuration is important.

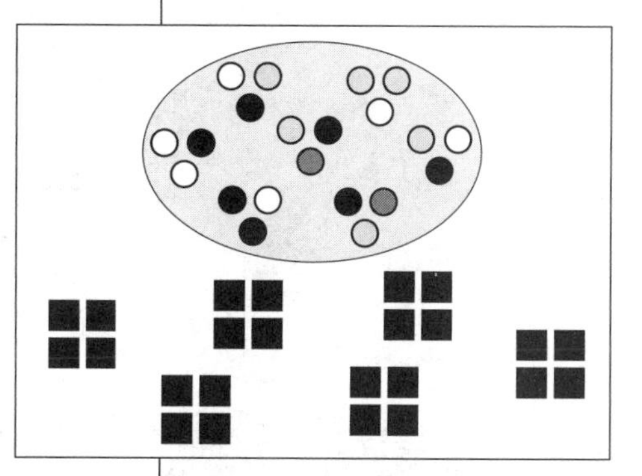

Lower-elementary students generally sit in small groups in the community area, with their knees touching.

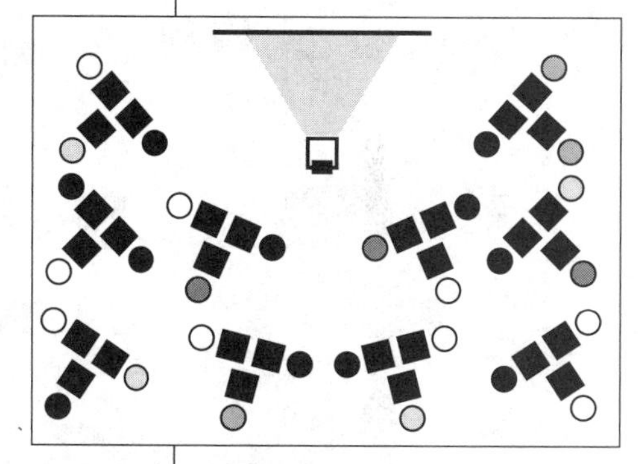

Upper-elementary students rearrange desks or tables into small groups, with the edges of the desks touching.

"Compliment specific behavior you want to see repeated by others in the next move. Children love to be caught being good!"

STEP 2 Give students resources that inspire critical thinking.

Imagine yourself in a heated discussion about an unusual news event, controversial song lyrics, or an intriguing human dilemma. The passion you feel at such moments is what every social studies teacher hopes to create during class discussions of geography, history, civics, and economics. The first step to fostering such lively discussions among your students is to give them something exciting to talk about.

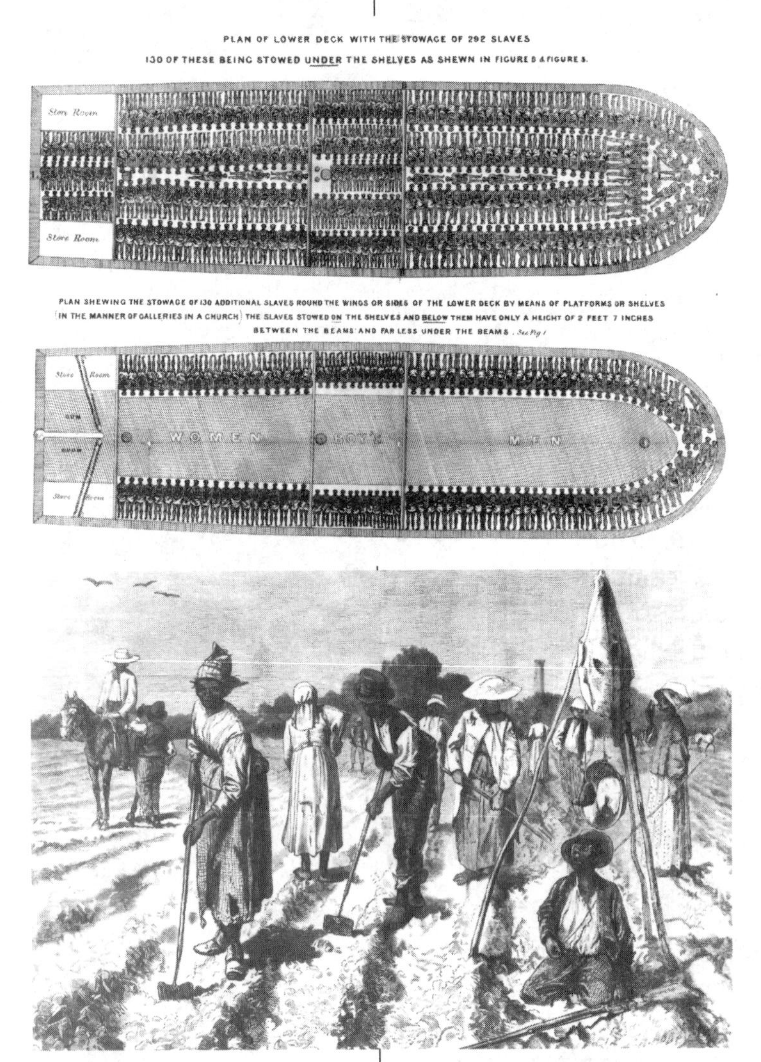

Compelling primary resources—such as the diagram (above) showing the inhumane, crowded conditions on slave ships and the illustration (below) showing slaves at work on a plantation—challenge students to think critically about the topic at hand.

Choosing the right resources for students to discuss during Response Group activities requires a keen sense of what excites students. Lower-elementary students are often intrigued with simple moral dilemmas. You could show a photograph of a child tossing a soda can into the bushes and have students debate which of these responses would be best: *(A) Ignore it. (B) Pick it up yourself. (C) Tell her to pick it up.* Lower-elementary students also love guessing games. To teach a history lesson, you might put students into Response Groups and project images of school objects from the 1800s (such as a coal-burning stove, an oil-burning lamp, and a slate) and have them guess the function of each object.

Upper-elementary students can be given resources that challenge them to resolve historical dilemmas, understand multiple perspectives, or categorize abstract ideas. For example, you might show a dramatic photograph of children playing in an impoverished area of Chicago in 1890 and ask students to describe what they would do to improve life back then. Or you might give students primary resources detailing the dilemmas West Africans faced during the slave trade and ask them how they might have responded.

Social Studies Alive! lessons use a variety of resource types—compelling images, music, photographs of artifacts, readings—to stimulate Response Group discussions. You can easily find additional resources in your own school. Consider video clips, information from the Internet, library books, magazines, and audio recordings. Before using a particular resource with your students, however, ask yourself these basic questions:

- Will my students understand the resource?
- Will they be interested in the resource?
- Is there anything controversial, enigmatic, or dramatic about the resource that will prompt heated discussion?
- Am I interested in the resource?

STEP 3

Ask provocative critical thinking questions.

Now that you've assembled your students into groups and given them some stimulating resources, it's time to carefully craft a question, or a group of questions, that will lead to true critical thinking.

Before you begin composing questions, recall Jerome Bruner's theory of the spiral curriculum. He suggests that when students are taught basic concepts first and then progressively more difficult ones, all learners can engage in higher-order thinking. This notion is often overlooked in the elementary classroom. Students might be asked high-level questions before most of them have adequate preparatory knowledge to answer effectively. As a result, discussions often end up involving only a handful of students.

This illustration could be used to inspire lower-elementary students to think critically about how humans use the elements in their environment for survival. They could be shown this image and then asked the following: *Picture yourself as having been left in this mountainous place, where there are no other people, houses, or stores. Work with your group to figure out how you could survive. How would you use the natural resources in this place for food, clothing, and shelter?*

To ensure success in Response Group discussions, think carefully about how to fashion open-ended questions that leave a lot of room for discussion. Here are a few examples:

- This is an object from a classroom of long ago. How might it have been used?
- Suppose you found yourself living on this island. How would you survive? How would you use the natural resources for food, clothing, and shelter?
- With your group, list foods from as many different cultures as you can.
- Which of these artifacts do you think were created by Native Americans living in the Northwest region of the United States?

For some questions, you might offer several choices and ask that groups support their answers:

- A new girl has come to our school. What's the best way to respond?
  - A. Stare at her.
  - B. Wait for the teacher to introduce her.
  - C. Smile and say hello.
- Pretend you are an enslaved African. How would you respond to the inhumane conditions of the Middle Passage? Why?
  - A. I would refuse to eat and would resist any help from the slave traders or other captured Africans.
  - B. I would try to organize a revolt by the captive Africans against the slave traders, even though I would probably get killed.
  - C. I would try to maintain my strength and survive the voyage.

"The children talk about these issues for days to follow."

Allow groups time to prepare their responses.

Once you have given students stimulating resources and carefully crafted critical thinking questions, small-group discussion can begin. (At the lower-elementary level, you will need to read the critical thinking questions aloud.) In their groups, students have time to talk about, refine, and (at the upper-elementary level) write answers to the critical thinking questions. They will soon be prepared to confidently share surprisingly sophisticated ideas with the class.

"If you see or hear a group using a particularly good discussion technique (like asking a quiet child for her opinion), turn your 'teacher spotlight' on the success and let the group shine. Other groups will quickly begin to imitate the spotlighted behavior."

Follow these guidelines to inspire animated, purposeful small-group discussions:

1. **Assign and rotate the role of presenter.** At the beginning of a Response Group activity, assign the role of presenter to one member of each group. (Students might be familiar with other terms for presenter, such as group speaker or discussion leader.) Explain that this student will act as the group's leader while the group is working together, making sure all members share their ideas, and will share the group's findings with the class. Rotate the role of presenter for each critical thinking question.

2. **Have presenters remember their groups' ideas.** Remind presenters that they will have to remember the key ideas their groups talked about. At the upper-elementary level, provide groups with a handout that lists each critical thinking question or set of questions. Challenge groups to record key ideas to share during the class discussion.

3. **Give groups adequate time to discuss the critical thinking questions.** Lower-elementary students will need one to three minutes to discuss each question; upper-elementary students will need three to five minutes. Circulate through the room to monitor group discussion. If a group struggles, approach them and ask some additional probing questions. Then challenge them to answer your questions on their own.

4. **Ask groups to use a variety of ways, not just verbal, to share their answers with the class.** For example, you might have groups present a short skit, use their bodies to create a human statue, or sing a rap song that expresses their answer.

Small-group discussion gives students the opportunity to develop their ideas in a supportive environment before sharing them with the class.

Facilitate a lively class discussion.

After groups have had adequate time to contemplate and discuss a critical thinking question or group of questions, students will be ready for class discussion. By this time, your students should have plenty of ideas they are willing to share. The challenge is to facilitate the discussion so that the different points of view are brought forth in a lively, engaging, and civil fashion.

First, ask presenters to follow these guidelines:

- When called on to present for your group, stand up and face the class.
- State your name and which group you are speaking for.
- Start your response by saying, "[Name], my group respectfully agrees/disagrees with your group because...."
- Speak loudly and clearly.

Lively discussion ensues after students have had time to prepare answers with their group members.

To begin class discussion, ask presenters from two or three groups to share their answers. This will likely offer the class a range of views on the question. To further inspire rich discussion, try these tips:

- Ask whether any presenters have ideas that are dramatically different from those already stated.
- Allow two presenters with very different opinions to argue their points.
- Ask a presenter who has not yet spoken to consider the ideas already mentioned and explain which point he or she most agrees or disagrees with.
- If the discussion brings forth only one point of view, promote deeper discussion by acting incredulous and arguing the unheard perspective.
- Challenge students to support their answers with examples and facts.

As the activity unfolds, expect more thoughtful and longer responses from presenters than you have experienced during more traditional class discussions. Lower-elementary presenters should be able to respond from 10 to 20 seconds, upper-elementary presenters for 30 seconds or more. If a few presenters seem to dominate the discussion, be sure to call on a different group's presenter for the next critical thinking question.

"The students were tentative at first with the discussion process, but soon they were off and running, leaving me to stand back and enjoy their thoughts and words. And they now see that everyone in the class has something to contribute."

Multiple Intelligence Teaching Strategy

Problem Solving Groupwork

Steps at a Glance

1. Prepare all students for successful groupwork.

Assign engaging, multiple-ability projects.

Give group members clearly defined roles and requirements.

Give groups autonomy and time to prepare high-quality products.

5. Allow groups to showcase their work.

Every elementary teacher knows the value of successful groupwork. When students work effectively in small groups—such as the second graders pictured above, who are creating a plan to improve a neglected part of their community—the benefits are bountiful: increased tolerance for others, collaborative problem solving, effective negotiation, more equitable interaction. But when groupwork *doesn't* go smoothly, such results as hurt feelings, unequal interaction, bickering, and worse are likely to be just as plentiful. While most elementary students have regular experiences interacting with peers—whether on the playground, at home with siblings, or in structured preschool activities—they are rarely taught how to work in groups effectively.

Problem Solving Groupwork activities are designed to teach students the skills they need to work together successfully in small groups, both in your classroom and later in life. During Problem Solving Groupwork tasks, students sit in mixed-ability groups to tackle challenging projects, such as preparing a dramatization of some aspect of history or creating a puzzle showing what good neighbors do. The projects require the use of multiple abilities so that every student can contribute. Each student has a well-defined role—such as director, script writer, stage manager, or graphic designer. As groups are engaged in the activity, the teacher serves as a resource and checks off the successful completion of several steps along the way. Afterward, groups present their projects to the class.

STEP 1

Prepare all students for successful groupwork.

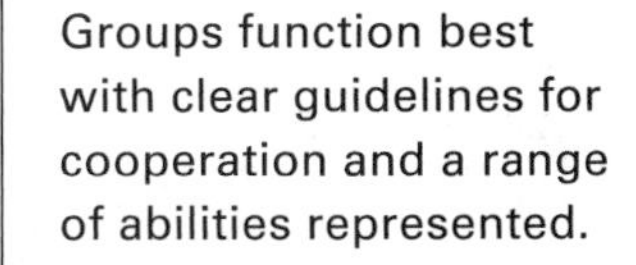

Groups function best with clear guidelines for cooperation and a range of abilities represented.

Many students have had few successful experiences with cooperative tasks in school. Students need preparation for cooperation so they know how to behave in groups without direct supervision. Set aside class time to create a new set of cooperative norms as discussed in Part 2, "Creating a Cooperative, Tolerant Classroom." While these cooperative skills can be applied during any activity, they are imperative to effective groupwork.

Once students have learned and practiced the guidelines for cooperation you expect them to follow, they are ready to join a group and begin a Problem Solving Groupwork task.

Plan to spend at least 15 minutes of planning time with your class list, assigning your students to mixed-ability groups. Balancing groups in terms of gender and ethnicity is relatively easy. And after you've had your class for a few weeks, you will have an idea of the social circles that exist and can use groupwork to break up cliques. The most challenging variable is determining predominant intelligences. The best way to do this is to observe your students carefully as they work on multiple-ability projects. To get a rough idea of your students' cognitive strengths, however, you might have them complete a simple diagnostic. (Examples are included in Part 2 of this book.) Use the results, coupled with your observations, to balance groups according to cognitive ability.

How to Work Cooperatively in Groups

1. **Smile, be friendly, and introduce yourself.**
2. **Arrange desks properly.**
3. **Use positive body language.**
4. **Use eye contact.**
5. **Listen to others.**
6. **Take turns giving ideas.**
7. **Use positive comments.**
8. **Be helpful.**
9. **Disagree in an agreeable way.**
10. **Follow directions and stay on task.**

Here are a few more hints for forming successful mixed-ability groups:

- A great way to help small groups work together effectively is to assign one student with strong interpersonal skills to each group and to make sure that students who struggle with interpersonal skills are evenly distributed among the groups.
- Note students' predominate intelligences next to their names in your gradebook or on a file card for easy future reference.
- Create a transparency of a classroom map showing where small groups are to work, who is in each group, and what each group member's role is.

STEP 2 Assign engaging, multiple-ability projects.

Successful groupwork tasks challenge students to use their problem solving skills to find innovative answers to complex problems, such as creating a human statue commemorating individuals who make a difference in their communities, designing a television commercial that promotes a city's positive aspects, or assembling a triarama (miniature three-dimensional scene) that depicts what families would need on a camping trip.

Nothing kills the enthusiasm and meaningful interaction of a small group faster than working on a simple task with discrete answers, such as labeling a map or matching vocabulary words to pictures. You don't need three or four heads to figure out answers to simple questions. If you assign limited tasks, be prepared for limited engagement and complaints about "boring" group projects. You do need three or four students, however, to tackle open-ended questions—tasks that are challenging and engaging enough to warrant the collective genius of several students.

Challenging projects that require a range of abilities—such as this panel debate between Loyalists and Patriots about whether to declare independence—help ensure that every student is engaged.

Once you've selected a task that requires higher-order thinking skills, you are ready to design it with multiple abilities in mind. *Social Studies Alive!* groupwork tasks are based on a multiple-ability approach championed by Stanford School of Education researcher Elizabeth Cohen. Cohen and her associates have discovered that the problem of unbalanced student interaction stems from status differences—differences in how students rank each other on scales of academic ability and social popularity. Students who are perceived to have higher status among their peers usually dominate group interaction, completely ignoring the contributions of their lower-status peers, who often revert to bad behavior or silent sulking as a result of being cut out of group interaction. To remedy this, Cohen suggests creating groupwork tasks that require students to use a wide variety of abilities so that all students have something to contribute and no one is left out of group interaction. Studies have shown that this leads to more equal interaction and higher learning gains for all students.

Before giving your students a Problem Solving Groupwork task, quickly analyze the task with these five questions in mind (adapted from Shulman, Lotan, and Whitcomb 1998):

1. Does the task require multiple abilities?
2. Does the task have more than one answer, or is there more than one way to solve the problem?
3. Does the task challenge students to use their problem solving skills?
4. Does the task allow for multiple perspectives?
5. Will the task be challenging enough to create initial frustration yet give students a sense of accomplishment once they complete it?

If you can answer yes to all of these questions, chances are the task will give your students a successful, engaging groupwork experience.

Give group members clearly defined roles and requirements.

After you have placed students into mixed-ability groups and made sure the task they are about to complete requires multiple abilities, one of the most efficient methods for creating smooth-functioning and productive groups is to assign each student a meaningful, specific role to perform—such as materials leader, building checker, clean-up leader, and reporter—and to give the group clear instructions on how to proceed. This will help ensure that all students contribute and will help prevent one member from dominating the group process.

This sheet clearly explains the group roles and the process for an activity in which groups of four create a television commercial promoting the positive aspects of a western city.

The key to creating these roles is to find an efficient division of labor so that each student is doing part of the groupwork task, and all parts of the task are positively interdependent. Each student will have a personal sense of accomplishment, and the group cannot produce a successful product or presentation without the cooperation of all members.

Once you have assigned the roles, make sure students know exactly what they are to do to complete their project, and carefully monitor each step of their progress. Let's look at how one Problem Solving Groupwork activity includes specific roles and discrete steps to help ensure students will succeed. During their study of regions of the United States, students are assigned to groups of four to create a television commercial about one of seven western cities—Denver, Salt Lake City, Boise, Seattle, Portland, San Jose, or Las Vegas—and perform it for the class. A student handout defines the roles and gives clear instructions for each stage of the groupwork process.

ACTIVITY NOTES 13

Step 1: Assign the four jobs for the activity.

__________________ will be the Advertiser.

__________________ will be the Artist.

__________________ will be the Salesperson.

__________________ will be the Director.

Step 2: Create a slogan for the city in your commercial. The Advertiser leads a discussion to create a slogan about your city. The slogan should summarize what you think are your city's three most outstanding features.

Step 3: Design a poster for your commercial. The Artist leads a discussion to decide on three pictures for a poster to be used in the commercial. The pictures on the poster should relate to the ideas in your slogan.

Step 4: Create a clear sales gimmick for your commercial. The Salesperson leads a discussion to create a sales gimmick to use in your commercial. The gimmick should make people want to come to your city.

Step 5: Plan your one-minute commercial. The Director leads a discussion of what will happen in your one-minute commercial. The commercial should be educational and funny. It must include the poster and the sales gimmick.

Step 6: Prepare to present your commercial. The Artist and the Advertiser work together to complete the poster. The poster should include your slogan and three pictures. The Salesperson and the Director work together to prepare the sales gimmick. The whole group works together to practice the commercial. It must be one minute long or less.

In this project, there is a clear division of labor: each role has a name and a list of expected behaviors. And because group members must work together to complete their jobs, the roles also provide for positive interdependence. Also note that students are given clear steps on how to proceed. Each step is initialed by the teacher after it is completed, thus keeping groups on task.

Give groups autonomy and time to prepare high-quality products.

Assigning students to work in small groups with specific duties and roles dramatically changes your role. No longer are you responsible for ensuring students complete the task and behave cooperatively. Instead, you delegate authority to them. They are empowered to make mistakes, assess their errors, and discover ways to correct them. It is your job to assign roles, organize students into groups, and monitor progress. You will also have to devise clever ways of helping students resolve common problems that arise during the groupwork process. Here's a heads-up list of problems you might encounter, with proven solutions:

Starting Off Right

When students first get into groups, have them do a team-builder relating to the topic at hand. A group about to create a billboard advertising the benefits of living in a particular colony in colonial America might, for example, take two minutes to discuss their favorite modern billboards.

What if one student is off-task or refuses to work in a group? Approach the group, and ask if they tried "two times" to include everyone. Remind them not to let any group member shirk his or her duties. To place responsibility for problem solving squarely upon the reluctant group member, and to communicate your expectation and confidence that the task will be started as soon as the minor problem is addressed, you might ask, "What do you need to get started?" If necessary, take the student aside for a pep talk. If all else fails, ask the group in mock seriousness, "You don't need me to sit in to help your group, do you?" Most elementary students, eager to establish their independence, will do anything to keep you from joining their group.

What if one student dominates the group interaction? Ask all students in the group to review their roles, and then ask, "Is one student doing more than his or her role? Is someone not doing his or her role?" Give them two minutes to discuss roles without you present and to decide how to better divide the responsibilities. Return to the group and listen to their resolution. If the problem persists, try to put the students into different groups in the future.

As groups work on the task, showcase positive student behaviors and attitudes. You will soon find the whole class striving to reach that new level of achievement.

What if students become confrontational during groupwork? Stop work on the task immediately and review the steps on how to cooperate in a group. Have them discuss a topic they are likely to disagree about, such as "the best" song or food, in an agreeable manner. Listen to their interactions, and offer suggestions for how to disagree amiably. Do not let them return to the task until you're satisfied they have learned to interact appropriately.

What if my class becomes too noisy during groupwork? This one you'll have to live with. Your class *will* become noisy, but it will be productive noise. If the noise level really begins to annoy you or your teaching neighbor, cheerfully ask the class to use their "inside" or "two-inch voices" and tone it down a notch.

What if groups run out of time before projects or presentations are due? Problem Solving Groupwork tasks generally take lower-elementary students 60 to 90 minutes and upper-elementary students 90 to 120 minutes (in two to four blocks of time). To make sure your students use their time wisely, however, you might tell them they have a shorter time to complete the project than you think they actually need. You can always tell them later that they will have additional time if "they make an extra effort to create a really great product."

Allow groups to showcase their work.

At the end of each Problem Solving Groupwork project, groups share their products—such as a panel discussion of the pros and cons of the American colonies fighting a war of independence from Britain; an enormous, illustrated map of a redesigned community; or a television commercial they perform extolling the virtues of a particular city. Here are some steps you can take to ensure high-quality presentations:

1. **Set high expectations for presentations.** Tell your students that you have heard about other students who made a similar product or presentation that was truly outstanding. Give juicy details about elaborate props or colorful artwork that was included in the presentation.

2. **Rearrange your classroom for dramatic, intimate presentations.** Clear a stage area in the front of the classroom, and ask students to arrange their desks or tables into a crescent shape around "the stage." Use the overhead projector to provide dramatic lighting.

3. **Have plenty of props on hand to make their presentations sparkle.** Think of ways students can use props (masks, posters, costumes, and physical objects) not only to make their presentations more dramatic, but also to put themselves more at ease. Many teachers keep a large box of props in their rooms for use at a moment's notice. You'll marvel at how creative your students can be when presented with a box full of simple props—towels, sheets, sticks, hats, colorful cloth, old clothes. Let them have fun!

4. **Showcase student products throughout the school.** Conduct a "gallery walk" in your classroom, having students view the projects and read accompanying explanations. Show off student work on bulletin boards in the halls, cafeteria, or administration building. Or display photographs of student work on your school's Web site.

Lessening Performance Anxiety

Acknowledge that students may be feeling anxious about performing for the class, and ask the other students to be attentive and supportive. As the first group assembles for their presentation, give a warm introduction and lead the class in a round of applause.

At the end of a groupwork activity, students stage a "wax museum" exhibit of figures involved in an economic activity that is essential to their state—in this case, the construction industry.

Considerate Text

Learning to read expository text is essential for academic success. You can support students by providing considerate text—reader-friendly text, structured with the audience in mind. Other reading supports include brief prereading activities, focus questions that set a purpose for reading, and the use of graphic organizers for taking notes.

Many a teacher is familiar with the chorus of moans and groans heard when students are asked to take out their social studies textbooks. If we relegate social studies instruction to the mind-numbing task of reading a lifeless textbook, we risk dampening students' enthusiasm not only for social studies, but also for reading.

For students of every age, one enduring challenge is motivating them to want to read. The TCI Approach meets this challenge by engaging students in "real-life experiences" in class—experiences that cultivate their interest in social studies, and result in students who eagerly turn to the textbook to learn more.

Additionally, the TCI Approach emphasizes the importance of using textbooks that adhere to the principles of "considerate text"—expository text that is structured to maximize comprehension by its target audience. Teachers know that learning to read expository text is a lifelong skill, critical for students' future success. With reader-friendly text, we can capture students' interest while developing a host of expository reading skills.

The TCI Approach recognizes that a successful reading of expository text involves four stages: (1) preview to set the purpose for reading, (2) read, (3) complete notes, and (4) process, or review and apply what has been learned. And even if your textbook is not "considerate" of readers' needs, the TCI Approach helps you structure lessons and activities to support readers at each of these four stages.

"[Considerate text] enables the teacher to work with the textbook rather than around it."

— Kate Kinsella, Reading Specialist

What Is Considerate Text?

In recent years, conventional social studies textbooks have become increasingly longer, cluttered with gratuitous visuals and excessive sidebar content. At the same time, more and more students struggle with reading skills or reading comprehension. Clearly, it is time to recognize the importance of "considerate text," a phrase coined by reading researchers to describe textbook content that facilitates comprehension. (Armbruster 1984)

Research identifies three characteristics of considerate text: clear structure, coherent writing, and audience awareness. These often overlapping features are recognizable in the following aspects of a TCI textbook:

A Clear Organizational Structure Chapters are organized in a straightforward yet elegant manner. Clear and comprehensive chapter introductions and summaries help students see the big picture during prereading and review activities. Headings are signals that help the reader mentally outline the content.

Comprehensible Text The single-column format, clear prose, and visual aids make the expository text easily comprehensible to young readers who are more accustomed to narrative text.

Elementary students first learn to read almost exclusively from narrative text. For a subject like social studies, we must use expository text that is considerate of developing readers.

"Chunking" of Concepts Each new topic is presented in a single, focused section, and each section is usually presented on a single page or two facing pages. Research shows that "chunking" new information in this way makes it easier for students to identify the main concepts.

Manageable Chapter Length Each chapter is dedicated to the exploration of a few key social studies concepts and refrains from veering off course with unnecessary features. Consequently, chapters are shorter than those in traditional textbooks. This helps students stay focused on the main ideas.

Careful Vocabulary Development Vocabulary is grade-level appropriate, carefully geared to students' prior knowledge. At the upper-elementary level, important new terms are identified with bold type and defined immediately in the margin. Such conscientious vocabulary support, supported by a comprehensive glossary, helps students learn new terms.

Clear, Helpful Images and Graphic Organizers Illustrations and photographs have a specific purpose: to lend deeper meaning to the text. When images are clear and large, and pages are uncluttered, readers are able to use their visual literacy skills to preread each section. In addition, text is supported by "graphic organizers," or images that contain visual referents for the main concepts being presented. These graphic organizers help readers focus on key content and make connections.

"Developing readers in social studies need a balance of expository and narrative texts at their actual instructional level rather than their frustration level."

— Kate Kinsella, Reading Specialist

How You Can Support Reading in Social Studies

Ask any group of teachers how many have students who are below-level readers, and you will see an almost unanimous show of hands. Many students struggle with reading, and most social studies textbooks are difficult to read. It is essential to attend to this issue and develop classroom strategies to help students with their reading in the content areas.

According to Dr. Kate Kinsella (2001), reading specialist at San Francisco State University, whose studies have informed the TCI Approach, "Learning to read in social studies should not be a 'sink or swim' challenge.... All students need specific coaching in a manageable repertoire of reading and thinking strategies for every subject area."

The good news is that you can help students develop powerful skills to move from "learning to read" to "reading to learn." Your first step is to create an invigorating classroom experience that will draw reluctant readers into the textbook. Many of the reading skills they need can be seamlessly woven into your social studies instruction. With the TCI Approach, you can give students effective strategies to help them comprehend and remember what they read.

Your social studies instruction needs to support students at each of the four stages of the expository reading process:

- **Preview** Include in-class preview activities and meaningful prereading assignments that allow students to preview key concepts and that motivate them to read.
- **Read** Give students well-written and engaging material at the appropriate instructional level, and offer graphic organizers that provide a focus for their reading.
- **Take notes** Insist that students take notes on their reading and that they use graphic organizers to structure the content.
- **Process** Wrap up each lesson with a processing assignment that helps students review and apply what they have learned.

The TCI Approach helps you support students' reading at each stage through Preview assignments, considerate text, graphically organized Reading Notes, and Processing assignments. The following sections include several tools and models you can use to help students with these four stages of the expository reading process.

Effective strategies and an invigorating classroom experience will engage and assist even reluctant readers. Here students analyze intriguing images of San Francisco to see how the city has changed over time, prompting them to want to read to learn more.

Use Short Prereading Activities to Build Schema

As you read in the section "Theory- and Research-Based Active Instruction," the TCI Approach adheres to the principle that instruction should be a carefully structured, spiraled experience, in the tradition of Jerome Bruner. Students begin by discovering how key social studies concepts relate to their own lives. Ultimately, they then learn how those same concepts apply, in ever more complex ways, to the world around them. Prereading and Preview activities are the starting points for this spiral curriculum and are essential for building the students' schema.

By *schema,* we mean the students' ability to activate relevant prior knowledge or personal experience as a foundation for understanding progressively more complex concepts (Keene and Zimmermann 1997). In *Teaching Reading in the Content Area: If Not Me, Then Who?* Rachel Billmeyer (1996) explains, "A schema provides a structure or guide for understanding. New information must be matched with existing schema so that it can be understood." Schema-building Preview assignments are an essential element of the TCI Approach. The examples in the "Preview Assignment" section of this book all demonstrate how these brief activities give students what they need to understand the upcoming lesson and reading. Following are some additional ways to prepare students for reading expository text.

The Preview and other prereading assignments build schema by helping students make personal connections to social studies content and concepts.

Prereading Prereading is a relatively quick, preliminary scanning of expository text in preparation for a more thorough reading. It allows the reader to create a mental outline. Conducting a prereading helps readers in a number of ways:

- They become familiar with the overall content and organization of the material before they begin serious reading.
- They establish a clear purpose for reading and a sense of direction while they read.
- They determine the difficulty level, length, and importance of the material so that they can allot a realistic amount of time for reading.
- They remember more of what they read because of the built-in repetition of key points.

One tool that helps you train students in the prereading process is a handout that guides them through this process. The handout illustrated below was designed for *Social Studies Alive!*, but it can be easily adapted for use with any other text.

Prereading a Chapter

1. What is the **title** of the chapter?
2. Read the **introduction**. List the two topics in this chapter that you are most excited to learn about.
3. Sketch the **graphic organizer** (if there is one) in the space below.
4. List the **headings** for each section in the chapter.
5. Look at the **pictures** in the chapter. Select the one you find most interesting. Write one sentence that explains how you think the picture relates to the chapter.
6. Read the **Summary** section. Write one sentence that explains what you think is the main idea of the chapter.

Anticipation Guides Another tool that can help build schema, the anticipation guide, requires a bit of teacher preparation. This is a prereading tool that also has value during the reading and the post-reading phase.

To create an anticipation guide, collect a series of statements about key concepts in the reading. The format is generally true-false, agree-disagree, or likely-unlikely. Students respond individually to each question both before and after the reading. This tool helps activate students' thoughts and opinions about content before reading, and then allows them to use the knowledge gained from reading to validate or revise their earlier predictions (Tierney, Readance, and Dishner 1995). Follow these steps to prepare an anticipation guide:

1. Identify major concepts and supporting details in the reading selection. Keep in mind what students probably already know or believe about that content.
2. Create short, clear declarative statements about the content, some true and some not. Five to eight statements are usually adequate.
3. Place the statements in a format that encourages anticipation and prediction.
4. Have students respond individually to each statement.
5. Lead a prereading discussion, taking a hand count to tally responses to the statements. Ask students to share justifications for their responses.
6. Help the class formulate a series of questions about points of uncertainty or disagreement. These questions will help students read with a clearer purpose and greater motivation.
7. Return to the guide after students have read the assigned text. Ask whether the reading led students to change their minds about any of the statements.

Prereading exercises allow students to anticipate what they will learn and prepare them to understand the assigned reading.

Anticipation Guide for Chapter 9 in *Regions of Our Country: Agricultural Changes in the Midwest*

1. Farming has been important in the Midwest for centuries.
   (T or F)
2. Farming tools and practices have changed little since the 1800s.
   (T or F)
3. It takes longer today to raise a bushel of wheat than it did in the 1800s.
   (T or F)
4. The most important new farm tool of the last 100 years is the tractor.
   (T or F)
5. More people start farms today than ever before.
   (T or F)

Predicting what will happen in the upcoming text kindles interest and helps keep students involved with their reading.

The KWL Strategy Another widely used reading strategy for approaching a new chapter, especially with upper elementary and middle school students, is the KWL graphic organizer (Ogle 1986). The three letters stand for the three responses students make before and after their reading: recalling what they *know* (K), determining what they *want* to learn (W), and identifying what they *learned* from reading (L). Again, the main purposes are to motivate readers and to allow them to elaborate on or amend their prior knowledge.

Here are the steps for employing the KWL strategy:

1. Set up a simple three-column chart on the board or overhead. Lead students in a brainstorming session of what they already know about the key content in the reading.
2. List what the students think they know in the first (K) column. Have students individually record in their own charts those items from the list they already know.
3. Elicit from students information that they anticipate they will learn from the reading selection. List these in the second (W) column. Have students list this information on their own charts for reference as they read.
4. Have students read the material, recording notes as they read.
5. Hold a follow-up class discussion, listing in the third (L) column what was learned from the reading, what questions were answered, and (in an optional fourth column) what new questions emerged.

The "Say Something" Strategy This directed-reading activity actively engages students in predicting and then confirming their predictions during reading. Follow these steps to use this strategy:

1. Have students read a selected portion of text and then stop.
2. Have students orally predict what will happen next. Write each prediction (with the student's name beside it) on the board or a transparency. Be supportive and encouraging, and refrain from refuting any predictions.
3. Have students justify and discuss their predictions by asking such questions as "Why do you think so?" or "What part of the text gave you that clue?" Encourage rich discussion by taking on the role of devil's advocate or by conducting a poll of the class to intensify the prediction process.
4. Have students read another segment of the text, searching for confirmation or refutation of their predictions.
5. Have students report what predictions were confirmed and summarize the most important information.
6. Repeat these steps until the reading is complete.

Guide Questions Writing guide questions is an easy way to establish a purpose for reading expository text. Simply change a chapter title and subordinate section headings into specific questions that guide reading. Then, as students read, have them look for answers to the guide questions.

Well-formulated guide questions help students focus their attention while reading. They also make the assignment easier to understand and finish. Guide questions that begin with *What, Why,* and *How* work especially well because they require a longer, more detailed answer. *Who, Where,* and *When* questions are less useful because they can be answered with a simple fact or one-word answer.

Here are guide questions that might be used for Chapter 9 of *Social Studies Alive! Regions of Our Country.*

With all expository text, establish a purpose for reading by providing guide questions. Well-constructed questions help students focus their attention.

Anticipation Guide for Chapter 9: Agricultural Changes in the Midwest

1. Chapter 9 **Agricultural Changes in the Midwest**
   Guide question: *How has farming in the Midwest changed since 1800?*
2. Section 9.1 **Introduction**
   Guide question: *What important information is introduced?*
3. Section 9.2 **Farming in the Midwest in 1800**
   Guide question: *What was farming like in the Midwest in 1800?*
4. Section 9.3 **Farming Tools in 1800**
   Guide question: *What were the main farming tools in 1800?*
5. Section 9.4 **The Farm Family in 1800**
   Guide question: *Why was life challenging for farm families in 1800?*

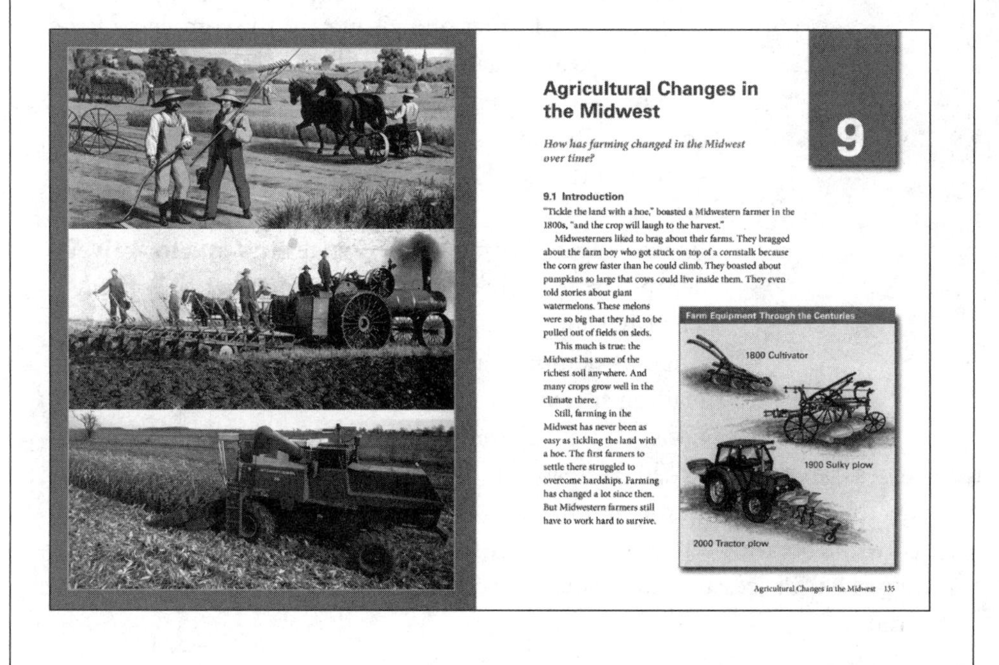

Agricultural Changes in the Midwest

9

How has farming changed in the Midwest over time?

9.1 Introduction

"Tickle the land with a hoe," boasted a Midwestern farmer in the 1800s, "and the crop will laugh to the harvest."

Midwesterners liked to brag about their farms. They bragged about the farm boy who got stuck on top of a cornstalk because the corn grew faster than he could climb. They boasted about pumpkins so large that cows could live inside them. They even told stories about giant watermelons. These melons were so big that they had to be pulled out of fields on sleds.

This much is true: the Midwest has some of the richest soil anywhere. And many crops grow well in the climate there.

Still, farming in the Midwest has never been as easy as tickling the land with a hoe. The first farmers to settle there struggled to overcome hardships. Farming has changed a lot since then. But Midwestern farmers still have to work hard to survive.

Farm Equipment Through the Centuries

Agricultural Changes in the Midwest 135

Use the Built-in Supports for Reading

After the Preview/prereading stage, other elements of the TCI Approach enable you to support the reading process without veering from your instructional plan. These elements include multiple intelligence activities, graphically organized Reading Notes, and Processing assignments.

Multiple intelligence activities motivate students to read for understanding. The greatest strength of the TCI Approach is that hands-on activities allow students to "experience" social studies concepts while using multiple intelligences. When motivated, students dive into their reading with unusual gusto. They learn that the reading will help them understand the "real-life" experiences they are having in class. This gives all students—especially those with weaker linguistic skills—a genuine purpose for reading. With purpose comes the motivation to read for deeper understanding. Use of a considerate text complements this process.

As students complete Reading Notes, they construct meaning from text. Even motivated, purposeful readers need strategies to help them comprehend and remember what they have read. In the words of a teacher and consultant on literacy and reading in middle and upper grades, "All readers, those who struggle and those who don't, need to be taught strategies that proficient readers naturally use to construct meaning from text." (Harvey 1998)

Readers of all abilities can be successful when considerate text supports the powerful multiple intelligence activities used for social studies instruction.

The TCI Approach helps students construct meaning from the text they read in each chapter by challenging them to complete innovative Reading Notes. As they read, they use graphic organizers—lists, maps, speech balloons, flowcharts, visual metaphors, spoke diagrams, sensory figures, matrices, timelines—to record key social studies concepts. In the process, they answer important questions, identify main ideas, make connections to prior learning, and synthesize new information. Ultimately, the completed Reading Notes serve as a visual referent that helps jog students' memories when they want to recall key social studies concepts. Examples of Reading Notes appear in the next section of this book.

Processing assignments challenge students to actively demonstrate their understanding of what they read. The final support for reading comprehension is having students demonstrate what they have learned. Many reading specialists will attest that end-of-chapter questions seldom help either the teacher or the student effectively assess what was learned. Instead, the TCI Approach asks that you challenge students to use their multiple intelligences to process and apply what they have learned while creating a personal product that reflects the depth of their understanding. The "Processing Assignment" section of this book contains examples of such products.

Graphically Organized Reading Notes

One of the most powerful ways to improve students' comprehension and retention in any subject area is to have them complete innovative, graphically organized notes on the reading they do for each lesson. Unlike traditional, outline-style notes, graphically organized notes inspire students to think carefully about what they have read as they record main ideas in a form that engages both their visual and linguistic intelligences. Graphic organizers help students see the underlying logic and interconnections among concepts. When students record information in engaging, visual ways, they are better able to recall key social studies concepts months—even years—later. Graphically organized Reading Notes, like Preview assignments, are recorded in the Interactive Student Notebook (further discussed in the section "Using the Interactive Student Notebook"). In *Social Studies Alive!* all levels except kindergarten have such a notebook for Reading Notes.

Let's see how Reading Notes function in an upper-elementary lesson about the factors that enabled the American colonies to defeat the much more powerful British army during the Revolutionary War. The lesson begins with a dynamic prereading activity. Students engage in a tug-of-war in which the teacher alters the rules to favor a seemingly weaker team, much as a number of factors ultimately helped the American colonies win the Revolutionary War.

Recording key ideas in graphically organized notes will help students remember content long after the lesson is over. Graphic organizers help students create a lasting "mental snapshot" of the most important information.

After the tug-of-war, students read a chapter about the factors that allowed the Continental Army to defeat the British army. To help them fully comprehend and retain the reading, students complete Reading Notes for each section of the chapter. The Reading Notes employ several strategies that P. David Pearson and other researchers (Pearson et al., 1992) have shown help students truly understand what they have read:

Activating Prior Knowledge Students use what they learned from their tug-of-war experience as a schema for understanding the reading. This enables them to compare each of the smaller team's advantages with those of the Continental Army. For example, they discover that the teacher's allowing other students to join the small team is similar to the colonists receiving help from their French allies.

Questioning Asking the right questions is at the heart of truly understanding nonfiction text. Reading Notes pose numerous questions for students to ponder, such as, *What motivated soldiers in the Continental Army? List at least three ways the British army was different from the Continental Army. List at least two challenges the British faced by fighting a war so far from home.*

These Reading Notes help students visually connect their reading with their classroom experience and read each section of the chapter with purpose.

Determining Important Ideas Reading Notes encourage students to seek out important ideas in what they read by asking leading questions and giving students relatively little space to answer those questions. In this way, it will become immediately apparent to you whether students are taking rambling, irrelevant notes or are pinpointing the most important ideas.

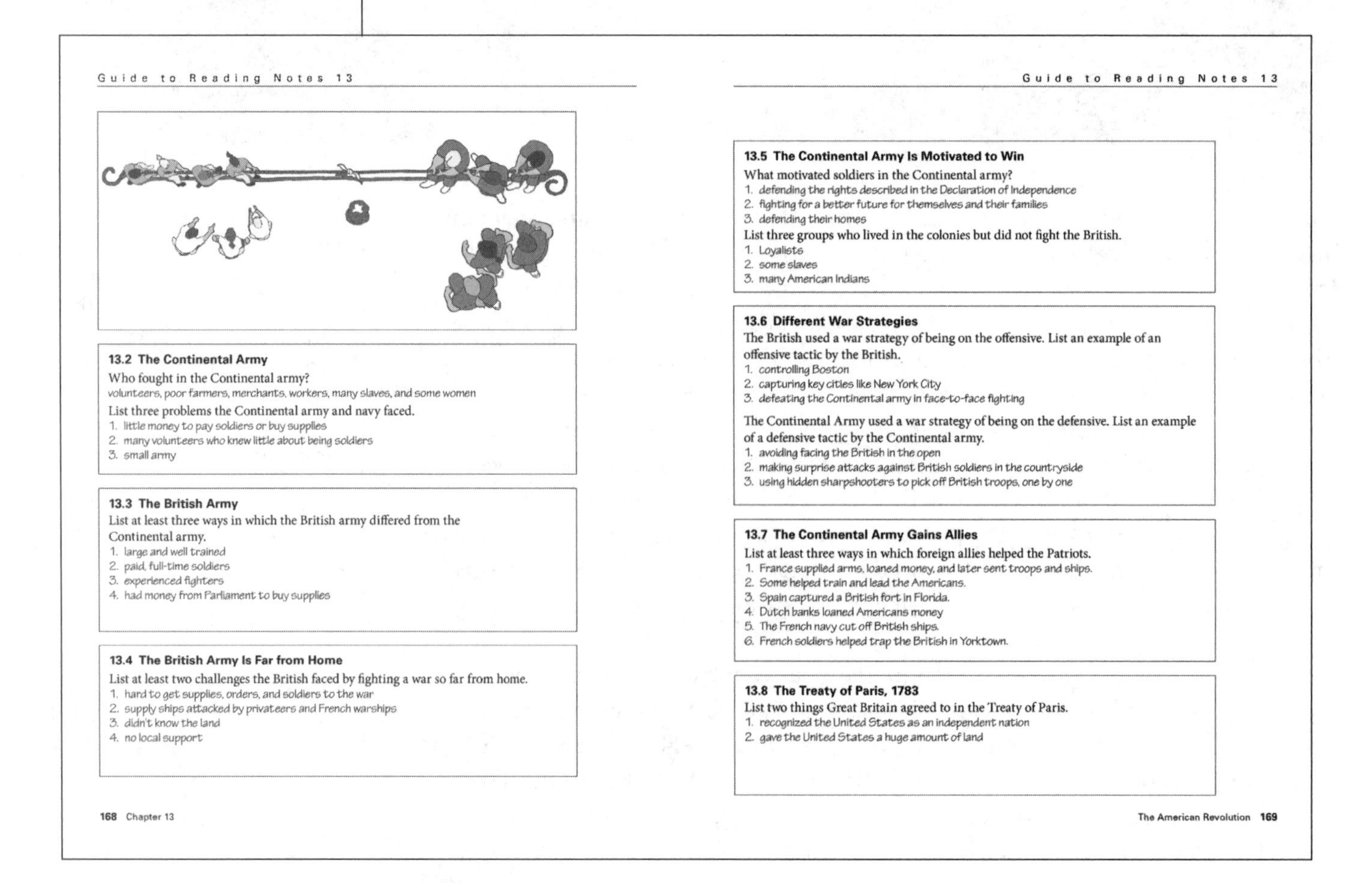
Guide to Reading Notes 13

13.2 The Continental Army
Who fought in the Continental army?
volunteers, poor farmers, merchants, workers, many slaves, and some women
List three problems the Continental army and navy faced.
1. little money to pay soldiers or buy supplies
2. many volunteers who knew little about being soldiers
3. small army

13.3 The British Army
List at least three ways in which the British army differed from the Continental army.
1. large and well trained
2. paid, full-time soldiers
3. experienced fighters
4. had money from Parliament to buy supplies

13.4 The British Army Is Far from Home
List at least two challenges the British faced by fighting a war so far from home.
1. hard to get supplies, orders, and soldiers to the war
2. supply ships attacked by privateers and French warships
3. didn't know the land
4. no local support

168 Chapter 13

Guide to Reading Notes 13

13.5 The Continental Army Is Motivated to Win
What motivated soldiers in the Continental army?
1. defending the rights described in the Declaration of Independence
2. fighting for a better future for themselves and their families
3. defending their homes
List three groups who lived in the colonies but did not fight the British.
1. Loyalists
2. some slaves
3. many American Indians

13.6 Different War Strategies
The British used a war strategy of being on the offensive. List an example of an offensive tactic by the British.
1. controlling Boston
2. capturing key cities like New York City
3. defeating the Continental army in face-to-face fighting
The Continental Army used a war strategy of being on the defensive. List an example of a defensive tactic by the Continental army.
1. avoiding facing the British in the open
2. making surprise attacks against British soldiers in the countryside
3. using hidden sharpshooters to pick off British troops, one by one

13.7 The Continental Army Gains Allies
List at least three ways in which foreign allies helped the Patriots.
1. France supplied arms, loaned money, and later sent troops and ships.
2. Some helped train and lead the Americans.
3. Spain captured a British fort in Florida.
4. Dutch banks loaned Americans money
5. The French navy cut off British ships.
6. French soldiers helped trap the British in Yorktown.

13.8 The Treaty of Paris, 1783
List two things Great Britain agreed to in the Treaty of Paris.
1. recognized the United States as an independent nation
2. gave the United States a huge amount of land

The American Revolution 169

Monitoring and Correcting Comprehension Reading Notes can help students learn unfamiliar ideas and vocabulary. For example, to ensure that students understand the difference between *offensive* and *defensive* war strategies, these terms are italicized in the Reading Notes, and students are asked to give an example of each. The teacher can then easily check students' notes for understanding.

Synthesizing Information Reading Notes help students review and organize information. A single graphic organizer, used to represent an entire chapter, gives students a bird's-eye view of the chapter and helps them see how information from one section connects to that of another. In the Reading Notes on the Revolutionary War, students can quickly see and analyze how several factors that favored the Continental Army combined to lead to the British defeat.

"The Reading Notes make so many connections with the text that the children's comprehension has increased dramatically. They have helped the children become more purposeful in their reading and in the completion of their assignments."

Visualizing When readers form mental pictures while reading, they are more likely to persevere with the text when it grows more difficult (Keene and Zimmerman, 1997). The visual metaphor of a tug-of-war is a powerful image on which students can "hang" more complex historical details. Such visualizing helps them better comprehend and remember tough expository reading.

Examples of Graphically Organized Reading Notes

Following are some additional examples of Reading Notes with inventive graphic organizers that will help your students process and remember what they read.

How Are Goods Made and Brought to Us?

Reading: Lower-elementary students read about how goods are produced in factories, transported to and stored in warehouses, and then transported to and sold in stores.

Reading Notes: Students label a diagram that shows the movement of goods from a toy factory to a store. This prepares them to complete a flowchart that shows how goods are made, shipped, distributed, and sold. They must draw a picture for each step in the flowchart and put the steps in the correct order.

What Is a Map?

Reading: Lower-elementary students read that a map is a drawing of a place. It has symbols and a key, and shows the directions north, east, south, and west.

Reading Notes: Students use what they have read about maps to complete a map of a fictitious teacher's classroom, locating the door, tables, cabinets, desks, and computer. They color the symbols and key as directed by their teacher to reinforce their understanding of the reading.

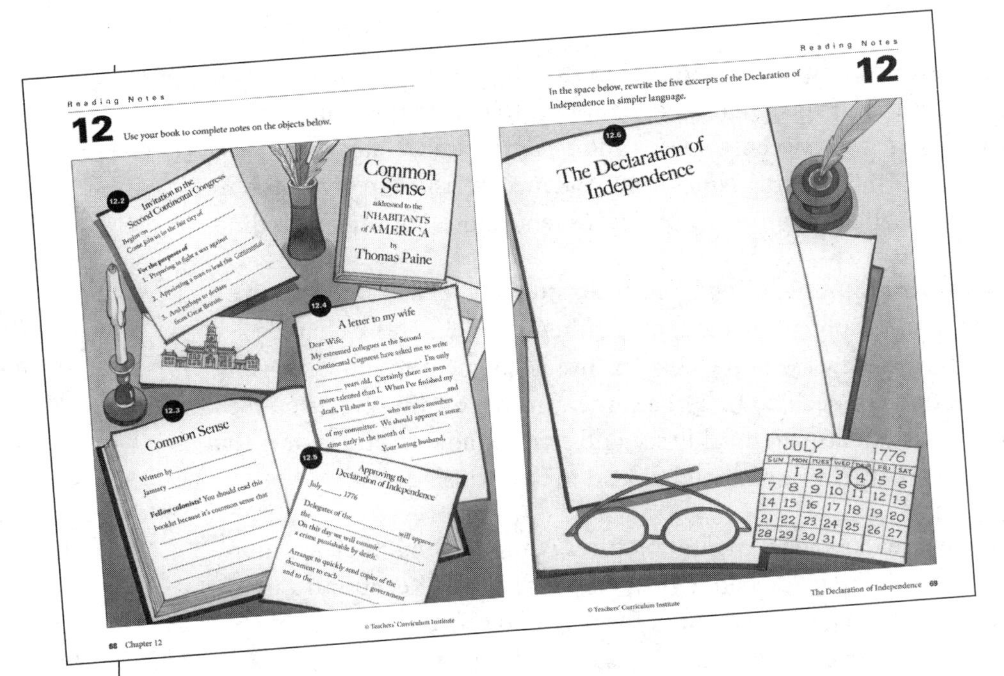
Reading Notes

12 Use your book to complete notes on the objects below.

12.2 Invitation to the Second Continental Congress

Begins on ______

Come join us in the fair city of ______

For the purposes of

1. Preparing to fight a war against ______
2. Appointing a man to lead the Continental ______
3. And perhaps to declare ______ from Great Britain.

Common Sense addressed to the INHABITANTS of AMERICA by Thomas Paine

12.4 A letter to my wife

Dear Wife,

My esteemed colleagues at the Second Continental Cogress have asked me to write ______. I'm only ______ years old. Certainly there are men more talented than I. When I've finished my draft, I'll show it to ______ and ______ who are also members of my committee. We should approve it some time early in the month of ______.

Your loving husband,

______

12.3 Common Sense

Written by ______

January ______

Fellow colonists! You should read this booklet because it's common sense that ______

12.5 Approving the Declaration of Independence

July ____, 1776

Delegates of the ______ will approve the ______

On this day we will commit a crime punishable by death.

Arrange to quickly send copies of the document to each ______ and to the ______ government

© Teachers' Curriculum Institute

68 Chapter 12

Reading Notes

12

In the space below, rewrite the five excerpts of the Declaration of Independence in simpler language.

12.6 The Declaration of Independence

JULY 1776

© Teachers' Curriculum Institute

The Declaration of Independence 69

How Do Leaders Help Their Communities?

Reading: Lower-elementary students read about how leaders help their communities by making laws, spending the community's money to pay for services, and deciding when and where to build new buildings and parks.

Reading Notes: Students use a vocabulary word bank to identify the types of decisions community leaders make, recording the ideas presented in their reading.

What Are the Social Sciences?

Reading: Upper-elementary students read about four types of social scientists—economists, historians, geographers, and political scientists—and discover that they offer powerful ways to understand individuals and society.

Reading Notes: Students create a spoke diagram for each social scientist. At the center of each spoke diagram is a hat representing that particular social science. Students attach words, symbols, and pictures to each hat to show they understand what that social scientist does.

Early English Settlements

Reading: Upper-elementary students read about life and hardships in three early settlements in America: Roanoke, Jamestown, and Plymouth.

Reading Notes: Students reflect on their reading by completing "sensory figures," recording details that a historical figure from each settlement might have seen, heard, smelled, tasted, said, and felt.

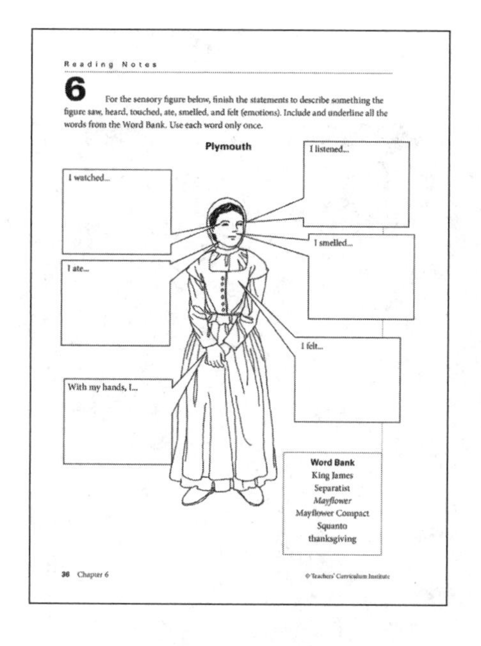

Reading Notes

6 For the sensory figure below, finish the statements to describe something the figure saw, heard, touched, ate, smelled, and felt (emotions). Include and underline all the words from the Word Bank. Use each word only once.

Plymouth

I watched...

I listened...

I smelled...

I ate...

I felt...

With my hands, I...

Word Bank
King James
Separatist
Mayflower
Mayflower Compact
Squanto
thanksgiving

36 Chapter 6

© Teachers' Curriculum Institute

The Declaration of Independence

Reading: Upper-elementary students read about people and events that led up to signing the Declaration of Independence, including biographical details on Thomas Jefferson, the convening of the Second Continental Congress, and the publication of Thomas Paine's booklet *Common Sense.* They also read about how and why the Declaration was signed and interpret key excerpts.

Reading Notes: Students analyze what they read by annotating a graphic organizer of the famous desk upon which Jefferson wrote the Declaration. They record notes by completing missing parts of several artifacts from Jefferson's desk. For example, they fill out an invitation to the Second Continental Congress, write an introductory page for *Common Sense,* and rewrite five excerpts from the Declaration of Independence, using their own words.

Whose Planet Is It, Anyway?

Reading: Upper-elementary students read case studies of how people have solved environmental problems in and around their communities. For example, they read about how a group of third graders in El Segundo, California, planted trees in their community to help reduce air pollution.

Reading Notes: Students complete two-frame "Pollution Solution" cartoons for each case study. In the first frame, students fill in speech bubbles for two characters, explaining what is polluted and how it became polluted. Students draw the next frame themselves, with pictures and speech bubbles in which the two characters tell how their community worked together to solve the problem.

Processing Assignment

Processing assignments challenge students to show their understanding of new ideas in a variety of creative ways. They often involve a visual product (a poster, a cartoon, an advertisement) or a written product (a poem, a journal, a letter).

In the TCI Approach, the Processing assignment is a lesson wrap-up activity that challenges students to synthesize and apply the information they have learned. As students work out an understanding of new material, they may explore their opinions, clarify their values, or express their reactions to lesson activities. Rather than simply reviewing their Reading Notes, students revisit the lesson content through multiple intelligences and higher-order thinking skills. By actively doing something with the information, making connections, and relating new ideas to one another, students will better understand and remember the content.

There are many different and engaging ways to help students process new ideas. They might create illustrations, diagrams, flowcharts, poetry, matrices, cartoons, or similar products. They might wonder about hypothetical ("what if") situations, or express their feelings and reactions to classroom activities that tapped into interpersonal intelligence. Completed Processing assignments usually have an appropriate title, use many colors, incorporate key information from the lesson, and show graphical imagination and creativity. At the upper-elementary level, students may use a variety of resources (the textbook, notes, outside readings, Internet resources, TV documentaries, and so on). For each Processing assignment, the main intent is to have students actively apply what they learned in a lesson so that you—and they—can assess their understanding.

Examples of Processing Assignments

Following are a variety of types of Processing assignments, with representative examples linked to specific content from *Social Studies Alive!*

Proclamation Scrolls In a lower-elementary lesson, students learn about ways family members care for each other. They process what they learn by creating "proclamation scrolls" that list ways they will help their families. They learn that a proclamation is a statement a person makes that tells what the person intends to do. Students create their scrolls by writing and illustrating a sentence that begins "I will help my family by... ."

Class Quilt In a lower-elementary lesson, students explore colorful family traditions and celebrations from different cultures, including a piñata party and a Chinese Lantern Festival. For the Processing activity, each child illustrates one square for a class quilt. They draw pictures or symbols of the foods, decorations, clothing, and activities that represent a traditional celebration in their family. When the completed squares are assembled in quilt form, children present their squares to the class.

Community Service Awards In a lower-elementary lesson, students learn about four people who made a difference in their communities: Jane Addams, who helped Chicago's children; Garrett Morgan, who made his community safer by inventing the traffic light; Susan LaFlesche Picotte, a Native American who helped sick people on her reservation; and Luis Valdez, who wrote plays to improve farmworkers' lives. At the end of the lesson, students create an award to honor another person who has made a contribution to a community. They share their finished awards with the class.

Postcards In a lower-elementary lesson, students learn about some of the products grown or manufactured and then shared across the United States—for example, apples, beef, maple syrup, corn, shoes, furniture, blankets, computers, and soap. For the Processing assignment, students design a postcard depicting something special about their own community.

Proclamation Scroll

Student Handout 11.7

I, Molly Beyers

will try to help my family by

weeding the garden.

© Teachers' Curriculum Institute

Lesson 11 123

Processing 11

Make an award for someone who has helped their community.

Award

Name: Liam Scott

Problem: Children didn't have a safe place to play.

Solution: He gave money to the city to build a nice park.

48

Sensory Figures In a lower-elementary lesson, students learn about how San Francisco changed from a small seaport into a large urban area. Students analyze images of San Francisco in 1846 and 1852, and then create act-it-outs to explore what life was like during those two time periods. In the Processing assignment, students create a sensory figure of a San Francisco resident from one of the time periods that they learned and read about in the lesson—either a sailor in 1846, a miner in 1849, or an earth quake survivor in 1906.

Real Estate Advertisements In an upper-elementary lesson, students learn about early English settlements in North America by analyzing images of settlements and creating short act-it-outs. Students analyze images of the settlements at Roanoke, Jamestown, and Plymouth, using the visual details in the images and information from the text to identify the reasons for settlement, the hardships endured by the settlers, and possible reasons for the success or failure of each settlement. In the Processing assignment, students are asked to decide whether they would prefer to have lived in Jamestown or in Plymouth. Applying what they have learned about their chosen settlement, they use both words and pictures to design a real estate advertisement encouraging people of the 1600s to move to that settlement. They are asked to include descriptions of the geography and climate, opportunities for settlers, including possible interactions with Native Americans living in the area..

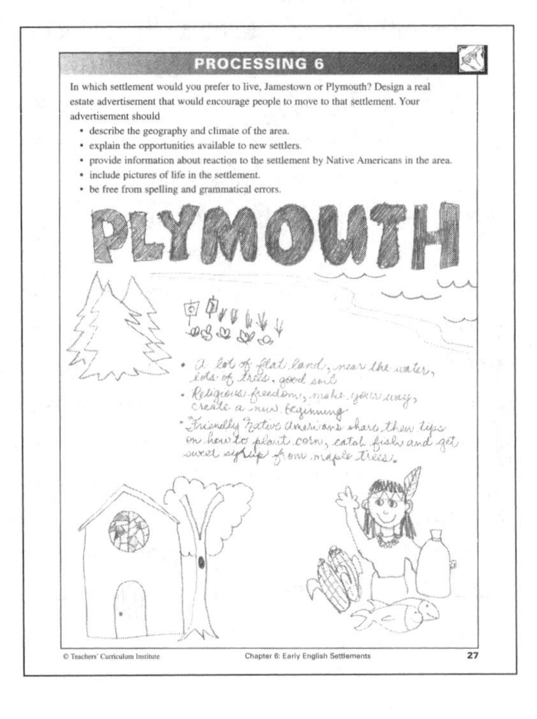

Acrostic Poem In an elementary lesson, students learn about community public services by reading about and analyzing pictured artifacts related to the police and fire departments, health care and child care, public schools, and transportation. For the Processing assignment, they write an acrostic—each line beginning with one of the letters in the word PUBLIC—that explains how public services help people in the community.

Travel Brochures In an upper-elementary lesson, students learn about the geography of communities around the country. For the Processing assignment, they make travel brochures about the geography of their own community. Their brochures include the name of their community and state; an outline of the state with a dot representing the community; and labeled illustrations of one physical geographic feature, one natural resource, and a typical day's climate.

Historical Eulogies In an upper-elementary lesson, students learn what life was like in the Union and Confederate armies during the Civil War. The Processing assignment is to write a eulogy honoring those who fought and died at Gettysburg. Students are told that a eulogy is a speech or a piece of writing that praises a person or an object. The Civil War eulogy that students create must describe the conditions under which Union and Confederate soldiers fought and died; must contain the terms *freedom, Pickett's Charge, trenches, artillery shells, wounded, hardtack, shortages*, and *Appomattox;* must be appropriately illustrated; and must be free of spelling and grammatical errors.

In the Civil War, in which Union and Confederate soldiers both felt they were fighting for freedom, conditions were almost unbearable. Soldiers on both sides often suffered from severe shortages of food and other supplies. Union soldiers ate thick, dry biscuits called hardtack; Confederates boiled chicory root to make a coffee like drink. During Pickett's Charge, artillery shells tore through the Confederate troops, leaving thousands dead and wounded. The Confederates finally surrendered at Appomattox Court House in Virginia in April 1865.

Public Awareness Posters In an upper-elementary lesson, students explore the history of water usage along the Colorado River. In the Processing assignment, they create a poster to educate people about the future challenges of water consumption in the Colorado River Basin. The poster includes an eye-catching illustration, a sentence that clearly states the challenge to residents of the Southwest, and a sentence that suggests what people can do to help meet that challenge.

Assessments to Inform Instruction

You can build assessment into almost any daily activity by observing and taking notes on students' work in class.

Effective assessment in social studies emphasizes activities in which students use their various intelligences to both demonstrate and further their understanding of key concepts in authentic ways. Such assessment reinforces learning and students reach a deeper and longer-term understanding of new material. They also perform better on standardized tests because the assessment focuses on cultivating a richer understanding of key concepts, not on test preparation itself. The TCI Approach supports the belief that effective assessment

- **Measures what matters most.** Evaluative activities and tests should focus on key concepts and higher-level thinking, not on what is easiest to assess.
- **Taps into multiple intelligences.** An array of different forms of assessment allows all students the opportunity to show what they know.
- **Involves activities that are indistinguishable from good learning activities.** Assessment activities should be both educational and engaging; they should involve challenging, real-life problems and tasks.
- **Fosters the habit of self-reflection.** Assessment activities should encourage students to evaluate their own work and to reflect on their own progress.
- **Prepares students for standardized tests.** Assessment should include some questions and tasks similar to those students will encounter on standardized tests, ranging from fact comprehension to skills application and critical thinking and writing.

Assessing Students' Performance During Daily Activities

Effective assessment begins with the assessment of day-to-day activities, which benefits both teachers and students. Regular on-going assessment provides timely feedback on the effectiveness of your instruction. If you can identify what is working for students and what is not, you can adjust your instructional plans accordingly. For students, you are sending the message that every activity is important—not just busywork—and therefore worth assessing. This regular feedback encourages students to apply high standards to all of their work. It also helps students identify their strengths and weaknesses in a safe, risk-free environment, and encourages them to reflect on ways to improve their future efforts.

"Standard pencil-and-paper short-answer tests sample only a small portion of intellectual abilities.... The means of assessment we favor should ultimately search for genuine problem-solving or product-fashioning skills in individuals across a range of materials."

— Howard Gardner

You can build assessment into almost any activity in two ways. First, when you begin an activity, take time to make your expectations for students clear and explicit. You can do this orally or in writing—or, when possible, by providing models of finished products. Second, at the end of an activity, allow time for students to reflect on how well they met your expectations, either by asking them to do a self-assessment of their work or by conducting a debriefing with the entire class.

Following are suggestions for assessing participation and learning in four of the specific activity types in the TCI Approach: Visual Discovery, Social Studies Skill Builders, Experiential Exercises, and Response Groups. Ways to assess learning in Problem Solving Groupwork and Writing for Understanding activities appear later in this section.

Visual Discovery You can assess students' visual literacy skills and understanding of key concepts presented in a Visual Discovery activity based on

- their answers to your questions during the visual analysis.
- their participation in act-it-outs that bring the images to life.
- the thoroughness of their notes in the Interactive Student Notebook.

Giving students regular feedback makes the assessment process a natural part of the classroom experience.

Part of your assessment for Social Studies Skill Builders might focus on each student's ability to work effectively with a partner.

Social Studies Skill Builders As pairs present their work to you for feedback during Social Studies Skill Builders, you can assess

- the quality and accuracy of their written answers.
- each student's ability to work cooperatively with a partner.
- how well the pair manages their time and stays on task.

Experiential Exercises After you have debriefed Experiential Exercises, you may want to assess your students on

- how well they met your behavior standards and learning expectations.
- their responses to questions during the debriefing.
- follow-up activities in which they connect what they learned in the activity to broader social studies concepts.

Response Groups During Response Group activities, you may want to assess your students on

- participation in group discussions.
- the presenter's ability to clearly express the group's ideas.
- the quality of their written responses.

How to Assess Groupwork Equitably

Assessing Problem Solving Groupwork raises many questions: Should group evaluations be determined by the quality of the final product or the process used to create it? Should each student in a group receive the same grade? How do you create individual accountability within a group? What do you do about the student who does very little but whose group does excellent work, or the outstanding student whose group does mediocre work? How do you keep track of the goings-on in all groups so that you can evaluate the groups fairly? What role, if any, should students have in the evaluation process?

Following are five steps for evaluating groupwork activities that address these questions. They give students a clear understanding of how they will be assessed, enable you to hold both individuals and groups accountable, and make the grading process equitable. One tool for group assessment, the Brag Sheet, is shown to the right.

1. **Set clear criteria for evaluation.** Tell students they will be assessed not only on the quality of the final product, but also on how effectively they work as a team. This underscores the value of using cooperative skills.

2. **Make both individuals and groups accountable.** Weigh half of a student's grade on individual contribution and half on the group's performance. Every member gets the same group grade; individual grades differ. In this way, students who do outstanding work in a weak group will be rewarded for their efforts, and students who do little but benefit from being in a productive group will not receive a high overall grade. Importantly, students find this system fair and equitable.

Brag Sheet

Name ______________________________

My role in the group was ______________________________

Student Assessment

My most important contributions to my group were

Our group did really well at

	not very well				very well
I completed all parts of my role.	1	2	3	4	5
I was nice and helpful to others.	1	2	3	4	5
I followed directions.	1	2	3	4	5
I stayed on task.	1	2	3	4	5
We worked out problems on our own.	1	2	3	4	5

Teacher Assessment

Group grade __________

Individual grade __________

Overall grade __________

Teacher Comments:

"Brag Sheets are lifesavers in parent conferences. Many parents are leery of group projects and group grading because their child might be 'held back' because of the other students, or their child could end up doing all the work. The students' explanation of their contributions help parents to understand the grade."

3. **Record notes as groups work and when they present their final products.** Observe groups as they work, and take notes on how well they exhibit cooperative skills and how each group member is (or is not) contributing to the group's success. Then record notes on the quality of their final product when they share it with the class. In this way, you can quickly formulate a group grade that is based on both how students worked and what they produced.

4. **Have students complete self-assessments.** At the end of groupwork activities, have each student complete a Brag Sheet, a self-assessment in which they evaluate their contribution to the group as well as the group's performance. This allows students to reflect on the group's effort and gives you additional information on which to base your assessment. It also gives students the opportunity to "brag" about their contributions—such as extra work done outside of class—so that their work gets evaluated fairly. Make it clear that Brag Sheets are confidential.

5. **Determine group and individual grades.** Use the notes you recorded during the activity plus students' Brag Sheets to formulate group and individual grades. Base the group grade on how well the group worked together (process) and the quality of what they produced (product). Record the group and individual grades on each Brag Sheet, total them, write comments, and return the Brag Sheets to your students.

How to Assess Writing Assignments Efficiently

Assessing written work can be taxing and time-consuming, especially if you expect to thoroughly review and grade every piece of writing your students produce. Here are some alternatives that will give your students substantive feedback on their writing while saving you from overwhelming paperwork:

Use peer-feedback groups. By having students exchange and review one another's papers during the writing process, you minimize the time it takes to review rough drafts. Consider providing a peer-editing checklist to guide students; one example is shown on the facing page. Reading one another's work gives students the chance to see a variety of individual writing styles.

Grade only final drafts. When students write both a rough draft and a final draft, you might give them some feedback on the rough draft, but actually grade only the final draft.

Use focused grading. Grade for only one or two specific parts of the assignment other than content. For example, you might look for an introduction that grabs the reader's attention, the quality of supporting details, a good thesis statement, a conclusion that summarizes the main points, rich vocabulary, strong writer's voice, or organization. Clearly define the criteria for assessment. Or, at the beginning of each assignment, consider *not* telling students which portion you will grade; this will encourage high quality in all areas of their writing.

Use a portfolio system. Develop a portfolio system in which students keep selected samples of their work throughout the year. After students complete several writing assignments, have them choose two or three to revise further. Thoroughly grade these "best" writing products. This is an excellent way to monitor individual student progress.

Stagger due dates. To manage your paper load, stagger the due dates you set for major writing assignments among your students. Allot ample time between due dates, and don't set a due date just before the end of a grading period.

Use a rubric. Create a basic rubric to allow students to assess their own work during the writing process. For example, you might tailor the form on the following page to reflect the criteria of particular assignments. Include space for both student and teacher comments. Communication and feedback is key to improving future writing assignments.

Celebrate Student Writing

Young children love to share their work with others. You might encourage them to give dramatic readings of their work. You might submit pieces to the school paper, display writing in the halls, or help students submit writing to the local paper or writing contests. And a publishing party is a wonderful opportunity for everyone to celebrate what the children have written.

Information Master 11.4B — Peer-Checking Checklist

Follow these steps to check your partners' letters:

1. Make sure the date is correct. If it is, underline it.

2. Make sure there is a proper greeting. If there is, draw a rectangle around it.

3. Make sure the first paragraph tells two important responsibilities that the writer learned about. If it does, put two check marks ✓✓ next to the paragraph.

4. Make sure the second paragraph asks an interesting question. If it does, put one check mark ✓ next to the paragraph.

5. Make sure the letter has a closing and signature. If it does, draw a ring around them.

Writing Assessment Form

Name ______________________________

Assignment ____________________ Date ______________

	Possible Points	Student Assessment	Teacher Assessment
1. I finished my rough draft on time.			
2. I gave polite and constructive feedback in my group.			
3. I used feedback to revise and improve my rough draft.			
4. I used social studies concepts correctly.			
5. I supported my ideas with details and stayed focused on my topic.			
6. I wrote organized sentences that make sense and help my readers understand the topic.			
7. I wrote my final draft in the correct format.			
8. I finished my final draft on time.			
9. I wrote all words neatly and used space between words and sentences.			
10. I edited my rough draft for spelling, grammar, and punctuation.			
Total			

Student Comments

Teacher Comments

How to Manage Assessment of Student Notebooks

The Interactive Student Notebook (explained in detail in Part 3) is a powerful tool for organizing student thoughts and notes and a good place to assess student progress. However, you must develop an effective system for assessing notebooks to keep the task from becoming burdensome and time-consuming, or both you and your students will become discouraged. The following suggestions will help you manage the load of assessing notebooks while still giving students regular, helpful feedback.

"Remember, students do what teachers inspect, not what they expect."

Informal Assessment

Here are some ways to assess notebooks informally on a regular basis, thus giving students immediate feedback as well as saving you time during more formal evaluations of notebooks:

Monitor notebooks aggressively in the first two or three weeks of the year. Glance at notebooks each time they are used. Walk around the classroom while students are working, giving positive comments and helpful suggestions. This is especially important early in the year as you establish expectations for notebook quality.

Check homework while students are working. While students work on another assignment, walk around the classroom and conduct a quick check of the previous night's homework. Give each student a special stamp or a mark, such as 0 = not done; ✔– = needs work; ✔= average work; ✔+ = excellent. This helps ensure that students complete their work on time and allows you to give them immediate feedback.

Set a clear, high standard. Provide a model of outstanding work for an assignment or set of class notes. Have pairs use the model to assess their own notebooks.

Allow students to use their notebooks on a quiz or test. This reward comes as a pleasant surprise to students who have thorough, accurate content information in a well-organized notebook. If they have done a good job with their notebooks, their quiz or test grade should reflect this.

A bit of personal encouragement and guidance early on will help get your students off to a good start.

Formal Assessment of Notebooks

Some teachers collect and formally assess notebooks every three to four weeks; others do so less frequently. Regardless of how often you assess, here are some suggestions for making the process easy for you and meaningful for students.

Explain the criteria used to grade notebooks. At the beginning of the year, clearly explain the criteria on which notebooks will be assessed. This may include the quality and completeness of assignments, visual appearance, neatness, and organization. Consider creating a simple rubric that identifies the criteria and how they will be assessed.

Stagger notebook collection and grading. If you use Interactive Student Notebooks in different content areas, do not collect them all at once—stagger their collection so that you have only one set to evaluate at a time.

Grade selectively. Don't feel compelled to grade every notebook entry. Carefully assess the most important entries, and consider spot-checking the others.

Create a notebook evaluation form. To aid in assessing the notebooks, create a notebook evaluation sheet and distribute it to students to fill out before they turn in their notebooks. Examples of notebook evaluation forms are shown on the next two pages. Use them as a basis for creating your own evaluation sheet. The first form has been filled in to demonstrate how you might designate which notebook assignments will be graded. Before using such a form, make sure students know the assessment criteria for the assignments—such as completeness, neatness, aesthetic appearance, organization, and effective use of color. The second form allows for a more holistic assessment of the notebook. Tailor the forms to suit your needs.

"Self-evaluation is new to most students. They figure once they turn in a paper, it is out of their lives forever. Asking them to take the time to evaluate their work forces them to reconsider some of their answers and choices."

Have students do a self-assessment of their work. When students self-assess their notebooks, it enables them to reflect on their learning and critically review their progress. Explain that if your assessment differs markedly from theirs—better or worse—they will have the opportunity to discuss with you the reasons for your assessment. Make it clear that ultimately your grade is binding.

Notebook Assessment Form 1

Name ______________________________

Assess yourself on each assignment listed. Also assess yourself on the organization and neatness of your notebook. Then I will make my assessment. If our assessments differ, you may politely arrange a time to meet with me to talk about the difference.

Notebook Assignment	Date Due	Possible Points	Student Assessment	Teacher Assessment
Preview: School in a Foreign Country	10/8	5	5	5
Reading Notes: Sensory Figures	10/15	20	17	18
Processing: Plymouth Real Estate Ad	10/18	20	20	20
Reading Notes: Comparing Colonies	10/26	20	18	16
Processing: "Goodbye" Lett ers	10/28	20	15	17
Preview: Dilemmas	10/30	5	4	4
Reading Notes: Facing Slavery	11/4	20	20	20
Organization		20	18	17
Neatness		20	15	10
	Total	150	132	127

Student Comments

I think my notebook is good. My Plymouth real estate ad was my favorite. Maybe more pilgrims would have come if they saw it! I also like the slavery lesson. That's why I think those reading notes are the best.

Teacher Comments

Overall, nice work. I especially liked the real estate ad, too. You blended strong visuals with a good slogan and represented the features of Plymouth well. Suggestions for improvement: Use a little more color in your notebooks, and pay attention to neatness and spacing in your writing.

Notebook Assessment Form 2

Name ____

Assess yourself on each of the items listed. Then I will make my assessment. If our assessments differ, you may politely arrange a time to meet with me to talk about the difference.

	Possible Points	Student Assessment	Teacher Assessment
Content			
• I completed all my assignments.			
• I gave my best effort on all assignments.			
• I used color to show key vocabulary and the most important ideas from the chapter.			
Organization			
• I did all assignments in the correct order.			
• I labeled all assignments correctly.			
• I cut and pasted material correctly.			
Neatness			
• My writing is easy to read.			
• My notebook is colorful.			
• My pages are not wrinkled.			
Total			

Student Comments

Teacher Comments

Give Tests That Involve a Range of Skills

At the end of a topic of study and as the last part of the assessment process, students should be given a culminating test that allows them to demonstrate, in a variety of ways, what they learned. Instead of simple fact recall, such a test should progress from comprehension of big ideas to application of social studies and reading skills, to critical thinking and writing. Accordingly, this test should include different types of questions and response formats. Specifically, tests such as these should

- tap multiple intelligences. Since traditional tests in social studies are purely linguistic, a more effective test should also tap other intelligences, such as visual-spatial, logical-mathematical, intrapersonal, and musical-rhythmic.
- include both closed- and open-ended questions.
- require students to do some form of writing.
- measure students' ability to apply both social skills and reading skills.
- contain elements found on standardized tests—like multiple-choice questions—so that students are confident when they encounter them.

Here, for example, are different types of questions from an upper-elementary *Social Studies Alive!* end-of-chapter assessment that concludes a study of agricultural changes in the Midwest. Though the questions represent only a portion of the test, notice how they collectively meet the aforementioned criteria.

Big Ideas

Fill in the circle next to the best answer.

3. McCormick's reaper helped farmers by
   - ○ **A.** killing off harmful insects.
   - ○ **B.** slicing through the prairie sod.
   - ○ **C.** cutting the time to harvest grain.
   - ○ **D.** planting seeds faster than by hand.

4. Fertilizers and pesticides help farmers
   - ○ **A.** become more self-sufficient.
   - ○ **B.** grow more food on less land.
   - ○ **C.** harvest crops faster than before.
   - ○ **D.** get higher prices for their crops.

6. What is as true of most farmers today as it was in 1800?
   - ○ A. They make a lot of money.
   - ○ B. They want to be totally self-sufficient.
   - ○ C. They must work hard at their jobs.
   - ○ D. They farm an average of 50 acres.

"These formal assessments really prepare children for standardized testing. Having been assessed along the way, when they reach this formal test, they usually smirk a little during the multiple-choice portion. 'Is this the test?' they ask. They have learned so much in the lesson that they complete this section quickly so they can get to the open-ended multiple-intelligence part of the test. They are truly unstressed about taking tests!"

Social Studies Skills

Use the illustration and your knowledge of social studies to answer the questions below. Circle the best answer.

11. The illustration shows a Midwest farm in about which year?

    1700 1800 1900 2000

12. Which tool would not be found in this farmer's barn?

    scythe plow flail reaper

13. Dairy farms depend mostly on which one of the animals in the picture?

    cow duck horse pig

Show You Know

14. Think about what you have learned about farming in 1800, 1900, and today. Choose one time period. Invent a tool or machine that might have helped farmers and their families at that time. Write a description of your invention that explains the following:
    - what the tool or machine is called
    - how it would be used
    - why it would be used

Draw and label your invention below.

"With the open-ended, multiple-intelligence assessment questions, the bulleted points tell students exactly what is required and make it easy for me to quickly evaluate whether a student has included the necessary elements. I also use this format as a model for writing my own assignments."

Upper-elementary assessments in *Social Studies Alive!* end with a unique, open-ended item that asks students to synthesize what they have learned in a personalized, individual way. This type of question (item 14 above) taps different intelligences and lets students show what they know in creative ways and in varied formats. Following are three more examples of this type of item.

Writing About Someone Who Made a Difference

Select one of the people you learned about in this chapter. Create a statue for that person by following these steps:

- In the space at right, draw a statue that represents how that person made his or her community a better place to live. Your statue must include that person and at least one other figure.
- On the plaque below the statue, write the person's name. Then complete the plaque by explaining what that person did to make his or her community a better place.

________________________ made
his or her community a better place by

Writing a Letter About the Southwest

Write a letter to a friend describing how the Southwest would be different today if dams had never been invented. Include these topics in your letter:

- How the geography of the Southwest would be different
- How the lives of people in the Southwest would be different
- How animals and the environment of the Southwest would be different

Add drawings to your letter if you wish.

Designing a Billboard About the Southeast

Design a billboard encouraging people to settle in the Southeast. Your billboard should include the following:

- At least four colorful symbols or simple drawings to represent characteristics of the region. Pick the characteristics that would most likely encourage people to settle in the Southeast.
- A short caption (two to five words) for each symbol or drawing that explains what the drawing or symbol means.
- A short, clever slogan that will help people remember why they should settle in the Southeast.

PART 2

Creating a Cooperative, Tolerant Classroom

Creating a Cooperative, Tolerant Classroom

This scene is repeated across the nation on the first day of school: students cautiously and self-consciously enter their new classroom, feeling guarded, apprehensive, and sometimes scared. Unless teachers invest time during the first weeks of school to change this awkward dynamic to one of safety, trust, and interpersonal confidence, the interactive instruction and learning described in this book won't prove fruitful. Students must feel safe and comfortable to share ideas, take risks, work cooperatively, tolerate differences, and disagree appropriately.

"Professional libraries are full of books about classroom-management and community-building strategies. Never have I come across a concise, teacher-friendly list of techniques like these guidelines. By following these steps, we are able to get down to the business of learning."

Using a systematic process to create a cooperative, tolerant classroom environment pays off with these powerful results:

- Students interact more freely—and learn more in all subject areas, not just social studies—because they are safe from ridicule, put-downs, and bullying.
- The class develops a sense of community and trust.
- All students feel valued and respected.
- Classroom management is proactive and consistent, rather than reactive and punitive.
- Students learn to tolerate differences, respect ideas, and appreciate diversity.
- You and your students develop a collaborative, rather than an adversarial, relationship.
- You and your students feel comfortable taking risks.
- Cooperative interaction is created and incorporated into whole-class instruction, groupwork activities, and paired work.
- Ethnic and cultural diversity is perceived as an opportunity, not a problem.

Ten steps for creating a cooperative, tolerant classroom follow. Use them as they appear, or adapt them to your own teaching style and the age and social-skill levels of your students.

STEP 1 Greet your students at the door every day as they enter your classroom.

Rationale Students like to be recognized for who they are: young people with a wide range of needs, interests, and feelings. Making time to say hello, smile, and talk with them demonstrates respect for them, conveys a warmth students quickly recognize, and models important social skills.

"Using this strategy changed the atmosphere in my classroom almost immediately. As soon as my students realized how much I cared about them as people, the rigorous task of discipline dissolved in an environment of respect."

What to Do Explain to your students that you will greet them at the door each day so that you can make a personal connection with each of them. Stand by your classroom door before class begins. As your students enter your classroom, model how to greet someone appropriately: make eye contact, smile, give a friendly hello or good morning, and shake hands. (During the cold and flu season, you may want to do "elbow bumps" or "knuckle knocks" rather than shake hands.) As the year progresses and you know your students better, your banter with them will become more informed and personal.

On days when you are unable to greet students at the door, assign a student to the job of "greeter" to welcome the rest of the class on your behalf. You may also want to stand at the door at the end of the day to say good-bye to students as they leave.

When Start the first day of class, and do it every day.

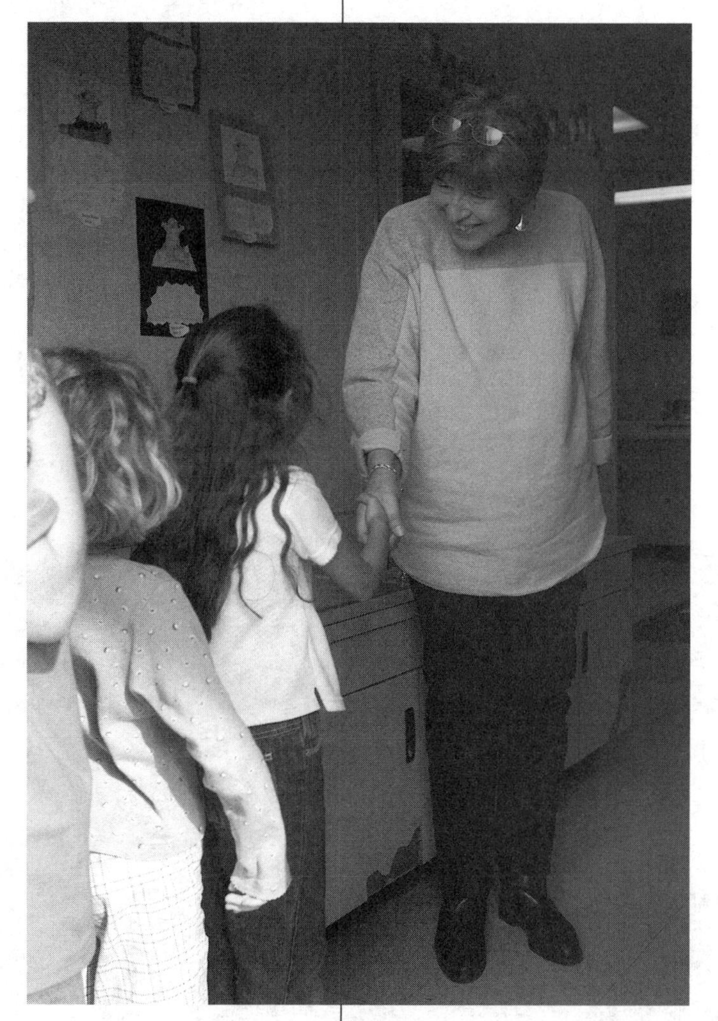

Greeting students as they enter your classroom makes them feel immediately welcome and sets the tone for a cooperative, tolerant classroom.

Explain your expectations for classroom behavior.

"I discovered a lot about myself as an educator when I implemented these guidelines in my classroom. Occasionally, I have failed to meet one of the guidelines, and a brave student has pointed it out. When my class realizes that I also must follow them, they really buy into the program."

Rationale The key to creating a cooperative, tolerant classroom is setting clear expectations for student behavior. Create a simple but universal set of classroom rules. You need not make a rule for every conceivable misbehavior— that only sends your students the message that you do not trust them enough to know how to behave properly.

What to Do Tell students that classroom behavior will be guided by a few rules, or guidelines. Explain that these guidelines are not intended to control their behavior, but will help them build a cooperative, tolerant classroom community. Here are three suggested guidelines; modify them to meet your needs. You may also want to involve your students in shaping them.

1. Treat everyone, including the teacher, with respect.
2. Use kind words and actions toward others.
3. Do everything you can to help yourself and others learn.

Give your students specific examples of respectful conduct, kind words and actions, and behaviors that facilitate learning. To describe respectful behavior, for example, you might explain how to share classroom materials or take turns on playground equipment. Then offer examples of actions that violate these guidelines so your students are equally clear about what is *not* acceptable behavior. For example, you might point out that teasing and name-calling are not kind actions.

Giving students clear guidelines for classroom behavior will help them learn to be tolerant and respectful.

Post the guidelines in the classroom, have students tape them inside their notebooks, and frequently review them. Most importantly, model these behaviors throughout the year. If you don't set a convincing example, or if your behavior contradicts the guidelines, your students will quickly ignore them.

When Introduce these guidelines the first day of class and review them every day for the first two weeks, especially as new students come into class. Review them every week or two during the year, especially as they relate to working cooperatively in groups (see Step 6 for more about working with groups).

STEP 3

Allow students to engage in an icebreaker to make them more comfortable with their new classmates.

Rationale Students are often nervous and anxious as they try to adapt to a new setting and a new group of classmates. Until they feel at ease, most students will not interact appropriately or be willing to take risks with one another. Many students, in fact, will not participate in class discussions until they are confident that their comments won't be belittled or quickly categorized as "wrong." As a result, it is crucial to invest time to break the ice and begin to build a classroom community. The sooner students feel comfortable, the sooner meaningful learning can take place.

What to Do Choose one of the icebreakers that follow, "Meet Someone Who..." or "Multiple Intelligences Bingo"; there is a lower-elementary and an upper-elementary version of each. Read the directions aloud so students understand how to participate. For "Multiple Intelligences Bingo," allow students to continue playing and shouting out "Bingo!" until you feel that your learning objectives have been met. After students complete an icebreaker, go through the categories to find out which students fit each of the characteristics. This allows everyone to acknowledge the talents, interests, and experiences represented among the students in the class.

When Conduct an icebreaker during the first week of class. You may want to use similar activities periodically to build and maintain the sense of community in the class or when new students join your class.

Icebreakers—such as having students pair up to talk about their favorite book or game—give students an opportunity to become comfortable with one another in an informal setting.

Meet Someone Who...

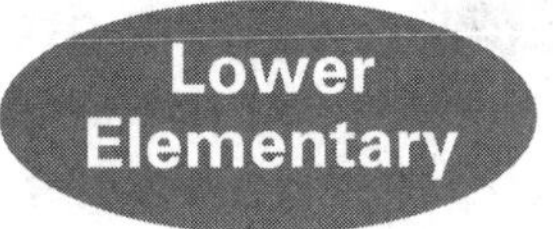

Find someone in class who fits each of these 9 categories. Say hello, introduce yourself, shake hands, and have the person write his or her name in the box. Each person you meet can sign for only one category.

Meet Someone Who…

Upper Elementary

Find someone in class to fit each of these 35 categories. Say hello, introduce yourself, shake hands, and have the person sign his or her name on the line next to the category. Then ask one question about the topic the person is signing. For example, for the first category about leaving the state this summer, you might ask, *Where did you go?* You can collect only two signatures from each person.

______________________ 1. Left the state over the summer
______________________ 2. Has shoes like yours
______________________ 3. Likes to watch shows about animals
______________________ 4. Likes to draw
______________________ 5. Has lost a tooth this year
______________________ 6. Has seen a play
______________________ 7. Has braces
______________________ 8. Is wearing jeans
______________________ 9. Has been in class with you before this year
______________________ 10. Is new to this school
______________________ 11. Is from a different ethnic group than you
______________________ 12. Has traveled to another country
______________________ 13. Has the same color eyes as you
______________________ 14. Likes to read in bed
______________________ 15. Has lived in another state or country
______________________ 16. Likes to dance
______________________ 17. Has a hairstyle different from yours
______________________ 18. Is much taller than you
______________________ 19. Is someone you have never spoken to before
______________________ 20. Loves social studies
______________________ 21. Dislikes social studies
______________________ 22. Has been surfing or ice skating
______________________ 23. Likes the outdoors
______________________ 24. Has more than five people living together at home
______________________ 25. Is an only child
______________________ 26. Likes to sing
______________________ 27. Speaks another language
______________________ 28. Likes the same TV show as you
______________________ 29. Likes to swim
______________________ 30. Recycles
______________________ 31. Has ridden a bike more than 10 miles in one day
______________________ 32. Has more than three pets
______________________ 33. Chews gum
______________________ 34. Plays a musical instrument
______________________ 35. Plays on a sports team

Multiple Intelligences Bingo

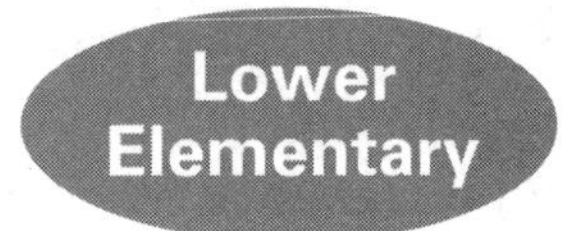

Find classmates who like to do the things below. Have each classmate write his or her name in only one box. When you have a row of four across or four down, shout "Bingo!"

Multiple Intelligences Bingo

Circulate through the room to find classmates who match the descriptions below. Have them write their name in the boxes. Make sure each classmate signs only one box. When you have a row of five across or down, shout "Bingo!"

Likes to work in groups	Is a good storyteller	Draws pictures a lot	Loves the outdoors	Plays on a sports team
Like to play chess or checkers	Keeps a diary or journal	Loves to play computer games	Is a good speller	Reads a lot
Listens to music every day	Can sing or hum a tune after hearing it once	Is a leader	Likes to work or play alone	Likes doing puzzles
Loves word games and riddles	Is a good artist	Has a hard time sitting still	Likes to take things apart and put them together again	Hums while working or playing
Can tell when someone is singing off-key	Belongs to a club	Likes to study bugs, plants, and animals	Wants to know how things work	Likes to do things their own way

STEP 4

Convince students that learning how to work effectively with others will benefit them throughout their lives.

Rationale Upper-elementary students sometimes need to be convinced that what they are learning is worthwhile, so explaining the short- and long-term benefits of cooperation may be helpful. (This step is important in most upper-elementary classes, but may be inappropriate for lower-elementary students.) Cooperative learning is not only a sound, research-supported pedagogical approach, but also a means to teach students valuable "people skills" that will serve them away from school, especially given our increasingly diverse population.

What to Do Make a transparency of "Survey of Employers," below. Ask students this question: *Other than being able to do the job, what do you think most employers look for in someone they are going to hire?* Allow them a few minutes for discussion, and then project the survey.

Point out that these top-rated characteristics—including communication skills, teamwork skills, and interpersonal skills—are not directly addressed in most schools' curricula. Explain that in your class, students will have an opportunity to develop those attributes as they work with others on a variety of activities. In this way, they will not only be learning social studies or math or reading or science, but also effective ways to work with others.

This step will take only about 20 minutes. Just make clear to students that you will be teaching not only subject-matter content, but cooperative skills that will also serve them outside of class.

When Do this sometime during the second week of the class, before holding any formal small-group activities. You may also want to send home to families a copy of "Survey of Employers."

Survey of Employers

Employers were asked to rank the qualities or skills they consider most important in the people who work for them. This is what they look for:

1. **Communication skills** How well do you speak and write?
2. **Honesty and integrity** Are you honest? Can you be trusted?
3. **Teamwork skills** Do you work well with others?
4. **Interpersonal skills** Do you listen to other people's ideas? Are you friendly and cooperative?
5. **Strong work ethic** Do you work hard and always do your best work?
6. **Motivation and initiative** Are you eager to get the job done? Can you get started without being told what to do?

Source: Adapted from "Job Outlook 2002 Survey of Employers," conducted by the National Association of Colleges and Employers

Teach students how to move efficiently and properly into groups of various sizes.

Rationale While it may seem unnecessary to teach students—particularly upper-elementary students—how to move into groups, a 20-minute investment will pay dividends in time saved throughout the year. Part of the success of group-work activities depends on groups sitting in precise configurations. Without clearly stated expectations about how to move into groups quickly, students can waste valuable time arranging the room, socializing, and stalling. Students must be able to move into groups and be prepared to work in no more than 30 seconds (upper elementary) to a minute (lower elementary). A brief training will accomplish this.

It may seem silly at first to teach students how to move into exact arrangements. But soon your students will be able to move into different-size groups quickly and begin working without disruption or delay.

What to Do Tell students they will be working in small groups throughout the year and must know how to move into different types of groups quickly and efficiently. Explain that before they move into groups, you will tell them (1) the materials they need to take with them, (2) with whom they will be working, and (3) where they will be working. As they move into groups, they should do so quietly. Tell students that you consider groups "in place" when everyone is seated quietly and properly, with materials ready.

Emphasize that *how* they sit in groups is critical. For example, in lower-elementary classes, if pairs need to talk to one another and are sitting on the rug, you will tell them to sit facing each other, cross-legged, with knees touching. When working in groups of four at tables, two students should be on either side of the table, side by side, so that students can face one another and share materials.

In classrooms in which students need to arrange furniture to set up groups, instruct them to use desks and tables already situated near their work area, rather than dragging furniture across the room.

Once these expectations are clear, create opportunities for students to practice moving into groups. For example, in a lower-elementary class, you might randomly assign students to partners, and indicate where on the rug each pair should meet. Tell them to take their social studies books and sit side by side. When the directions are clear, say "Go!" Time them, and watch that their movement meets your expectations. If necessary, explain what went wrong and have them repeat the process until they can do it up to your standards and in "record time."

"After I took time to teach Desk Olympics, my students can now enter the room, read the map posted on the board, efficiently move all the desks into the new arrangement, find their designated spots, mark their attendance and lunch count, and be ready to start class by 9:05."

Make the practice as much fun as possible. Some teachers call this the "Desk Olympics" and create various events, such as "Side-by-Side Pairs" and "Groups of Four." These teachers post "Olympic records" for groups to beat, and play the Olympic theme music before each competition. Even as students get caught up in the fun and competition, they internalize expectations for moving into groups.

When Do this during the second or third week of the class, before you do any formal groupwork.

Use role-playing activities to teach your students cooperative skills.

Rationale For groups to function cooperatively, students must know what it means to work in a cooperative fashion. While most students have regular experiences interacting with peers—on the playground, at home with siblings, or in after-school activities—they are rarely taught explicit skills for cooperative interaction. As a result, you must teach these skills or you will find yourself continually reacting to inappropriate behavior as students work in groups.

What to Do Create a poster listing cooperative behaviors, and post it in a prominent place in the classroom (see the opposite page for ideas). Then follow this five-step process for teaching each skill to students so that they have a clear idea of how to work in groups. For example, here is how to teach "Use positive comments" (Cooperative Skill 7 from the upper-elementary list):

1. **Name the behavior.** On the board, overhead projector, a large piece of butcher paper, or tagboard, write, *Use positive comments.*
2. **Demonstrate the behavior.** Have three volunteers join you in the middle of the room. Ask the group to generate a list of the five best presents to give friends on their birthdays. While they are interacting, encourage everyone to participate and praise group members who come up with good ideas.
3. **Define the behavior.** Below the heading *Use positive comments,* make a T-chart with two columns, "Looks Like" and "Sounds Like." Ask students to identify actions you took and words you said that were positive, and list them on the chart. Here are possible entries:

Looks Like	Sounds Like
Made eye contact	Great idea!
Smiled and leaned forward	Right!
Nodded head	Please repeat that so everyone can hear.
Gave "thumbs-up" sign	Thanks.
Gave high-five to group member	Do you have any other good ideas?

Role-playing with your students allows them to see cooperative skills in action.

4. **Practice the behavior.** Once students have clearly defined the behavior, give them a simple discussion task and allow them to practice in groups. Circulate through the room to observe their interaction.
5. **Process the students' experience.** This is where the most lasting learning takes place. Allow students to share their experiences before you comment on what you observed. Ask, *How did you feel when the people in your group used positive comments toward you? How did it feel to express positive ideas? How did using this skill affect your group's ability to work together? Why do you think this is an important cooperative skill?*

This process can be used for any cooperative skill. Observe your students to assess their cooperative ability. Depending on the time you have and your students' social skills, you may want to use this process for only the more difficult skills.

When Teach cooperative skills before students begin working in groups. You can teach these skills over several sessions.

How to Work Cooperatively in Groups

Lower Elementary

1. Smile, be friendly, and introduce yourself.
2. Sit properly.
3. Look at the person talking.
4. Listen.
5. Take turns.
6. Be helpful and nice.
7. Work out problems on your own.
8. Follow directions and stay on task.

How to Work Cooperatively in Groups

Upper Elementary

1. Smile, be friendly, and introduce yourself.
2. Arrange desks properly.
3. Use positive body language.
4. Use eye contact.
5. Listen to others.
6. Take turns giving ideas.
7. Use positive comments.
8. Be helpful.
9. Disagree in an agreeable way.
10. Follow directions and stay on task.

Form mixed-ability groups.

"I record the results of my multiple intelligence exercises and observations in the front of my lesson plan book so that it is easy to refer to when I plan groupwork lessons and reflect on how a particular groupwork lesson went."

Rationale If students are properly placed in mixed-ability, or heterogeneous, groups for challenging groupwork assignments, several common classroom dilemmas can be solved. First, you expose all students to high-level content because they benefit from the collective talent of the group. Second, you break social cliques and foster intercultural understanding. Third, you give students the skills they will eventually need to be able to work with different kinds of people in school, in community groups, and on teams.

What to Do No matter what size small groups you create—groups of two, three, or four—it is imperative that each is as balanced as possible in terms of gender, ethnicity, intelligences (as defined by Howard Gardner), and social group. Keep in mind that your ability to create smooth-functioning groups will improve with each groupwork activity.

Plan to spend about 15 minutes of planning time, with your class list, assigning your students to mixed-ability groups. Balancing groups in terms of gender and ethnicity is relatively easy. And after having students together for a short while, you will have an idea of the social circles that exist.

The greatest challenge is determining predominant intelligences. The best way is by careful observation throughout the school year. To get a rough idea of your students' cognitive strengths, however, give the simple diagnostic "Where Does Your Intelligence Lie?" (on the opposite page; the scoring key appears on page 114). With lower-elementary students, project a transparency of the diagnostic, read each statement, and lead students to complete it. Use the results, coupled with your observations, to balance groups according to Gardner's list of intelligences.

Working in mixed-ability groups will help your students take responsibility for their own learning.

Emphasize to students that the diagnostic is rough and does not suggest that they are only capable in their predominant intelligences. Also explain that people's intelligences evolve and change over time.

Depending on the success of the groups you create, you may want to have students remain in the same groups for several activities. Or you may want to switch groups to give students a change of pace or to try to create more effective groups.

When Assign students to groups before their first groupwork activity and after you have completed Steps 1 through 6.

Where Does Your Intelligence Lie?

Read each statement. If it sounds true for the most part, jot down a T for true. If it doesn't, mark an F. If a statement is sometimes true and sometimes false, leave it blank.

1. ______ I'd rather draw a map than give someone directions out loud.
2. ______ If I am angry or happy, I sometimes know why.
3. ______ I can play a musical instrument.
4. ______ I like to sing songs and raps.
5. ______ I can add or multiply quickly in my head.
6. ______ I help friends work out their problems and feelings.
7. ______ I like to work with calculators and computers.
8. ______ I learn new dance steps fast.
9. ______ It's easy for me to say what I think in an argument.
10. ______ I like listening to speakers talk.
11. ______ I find my way easily in malls and new places without getting lost.
12. ______ I like to be with friends at parties.
13. ______ I like to listen to music as often as possible.
14. ______ I always understand the drawings that come with new toys.
15. ______ I like to work puzzles and play games.
16. ______ Learning how to ride a bike (or to skate) was easy.
17. ______ I get upset when I hear an argument that doesn't make sense.
18. ______ I can talk friends into changing their minds.
19. ______ I have great balance.
20. ______ I see patterns and relationships in numbers quickly.
21. ______ I enjoy building things with wood and nails.
22. ______ I like word games and jokes.
23. ______ I can look at an object one way and see it turned sideways or backward just as easily.
24. ______ I like to tap out rhythms with my hands.
25. ______ I like to work with numbers.
26. ______ I like to sit quietly and think about my feelings.
27. ______ I enjoy looking at the shapes of buildings.
28. ______ I like to hum, whistle, or sing when I'm alone.
29. ______ I'm good at sports.
30. ______ I enjoy writing letters to friends.
31. ______ I can always tell what look is on my face.
32. ______ I can tell how people feel by the looks on their faces.
33. ______ I usually know how I feel.
34. ______ I can usually tell what kind of mood other people are in.
35. ______ I can usually tell what others think of me.

Scoring "Where Does Your Intelligence Lie?"

Put an X in the box for each item you marked with a T. Add up the number of X's. A total of four X's in any category indicates strong ability.

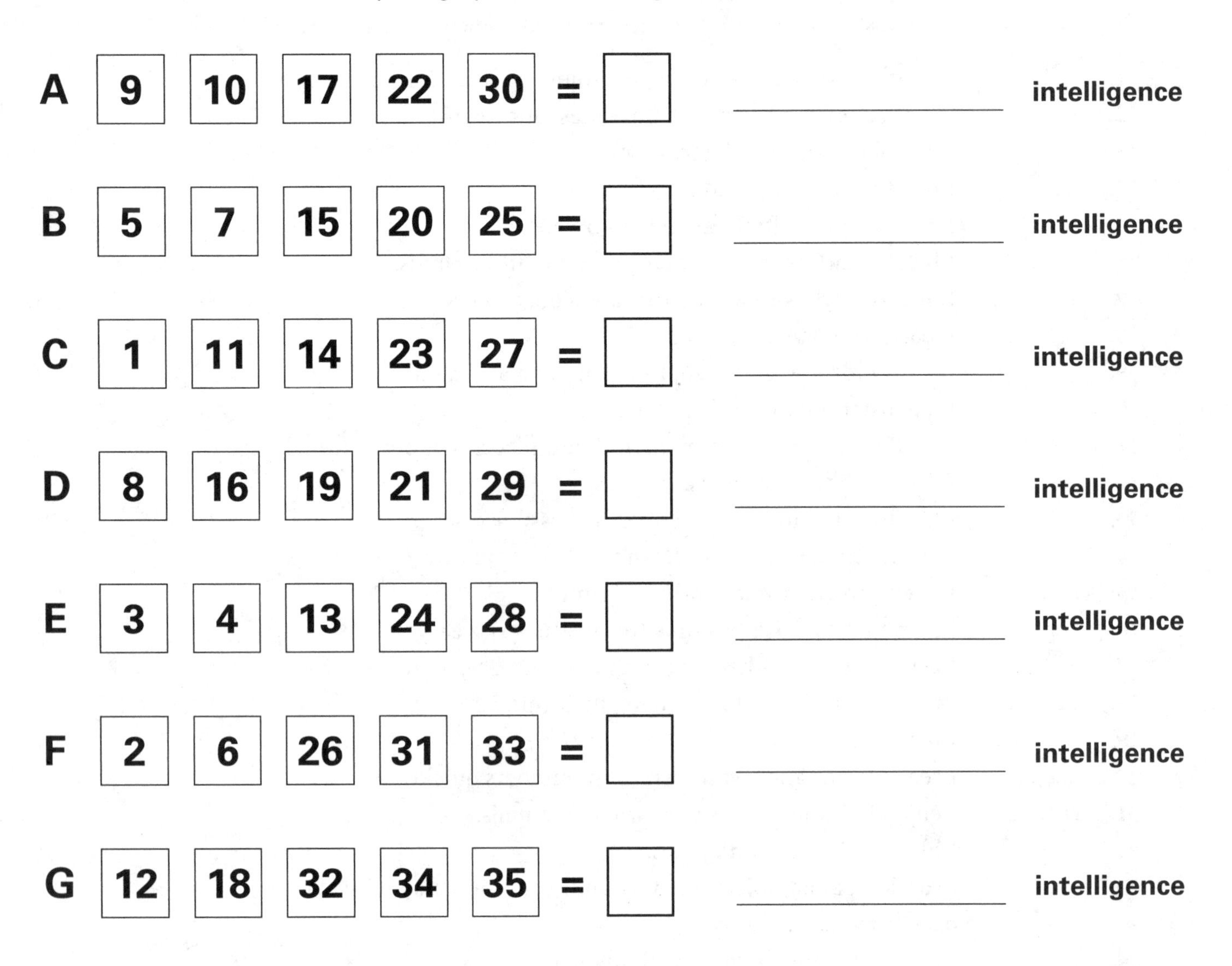

A	9	10	17	22	30	=	☐	________ intelligence
B	5	7	15	20	25	=	☐	________ intelligence
C	1	11	14	23	27	=	☐	________ intelligence
D	8	16	19	21	29	=	☐	________ intelligence
E	3	4	13	24	28	=	☐	________ intelligence
F	2	6	26	31	33	=	☐	________ intelligence
G	12	18	32	34	35	=	☐	________ intelligence

Teacher Answer Key

Note: Do not reveal these to students until after they have scored their diagnostics.

A = verbal-linguistic ("word smart")

B = logical-mathematical ("number smart")

C = visual-spatial ("picture smart")

D = body-kinesthetic ("body smart")

E = musical-rhythmic ("music smart")

F = intrapersonal ("self smart")

G = interpersonal ("people smart")

STEP 8 Allow newly formed groups to engage in team-building activities to help students feel comfortable working together and to build cohesive groups.

Rationale Before students can effectively engage in groupwork activities, they must feel comfortable with their group members and believe in the value of teamwork. It is imperative that team-building activities—exercises designed to create a more comfortable, cohesive group environment—precede groupwork tasks. The investment in time—5 to 30 minutes—pays off in opportunities for students to interact safely, to get a feel for the interpersonal dynamics within the group, to break social tension, to value teamwork, and to feel at ease working together.

What to Do Once you have created mixed-ability groups and have taught students how to move into groups, you are ready to have students join their groups. Follow this procedure:

1. **Once students are in their groups, explain that they will be doing a team-building activity.** The activity is designed to help them see the importance of teamwork and feel more comfortable with their group members.
2. **Give each student a copy of the team-builder handout.** For lower-elementary students, use "Going Camping" (see page 118; answers are on page 120); for upper-elementary students, use "Lost on the Moon" (see page 119; answers are on page 120). Read the scenario and the directions aloud, and answer any questions. Emphasize that students are to devise answers to Phase 1 entirely on their own and that there should be no talking until they have all completed their individual rankings. This should take 5 to 15 minutes.

Team-building activities help students feel at ease in their group and strengthen their ability to work as a team.

3. **Now allow groups to begin working on Phase 2, the team rankings.** Encourage students to use their cooperative skills while coming up with a group solution. You may want to display a copy of "How to Work Cooperatively in Groups," from page 111, as a reminder. As students exchange probable solutions, there may be heated discussion. That is okay. If students within a group cannot agree, remind them of the directions: they are to decide on the rankings that "best satisfy" all members. Expect that some groups will finish within 10 minutes, while others may take longer.
4. **After all groups have completed Phase 2, reveal the answers.** With lower-elementary students, read the answers while students write them in the correct columns. Explain the rationale for each ranking. Then collect the handouts and calculate the error points for individual and group rankings by finding the absolute difference between each pair of numbers. In almost all cases, the total number of error points will be significantly lower for the group rankings than for the individual rankings, supporting the notion that teamwork is valuable.

With upper-elementary students, read NASA's rankings while students write them in the correct columns. Explain NASA's rationale for each ranking. Have students compute the error points for both individual and group rankings by subtracting the lesser number from the greater in each pair of numbers. For example, if a student's ranking is 5 and the experts' ranking is 7, the error points would be 7 – 5 = 2. Similarly, if a student's ranking is 5 and the experts' ranking is 3, the error points would be 5 – 3 = 2.

5. **Hold a class discussion.** Center the discussion on these questions: *Were your answers more accurate when you worked individually or as a group? Why do you think so? In what ways can working together be helpful? When working in your group, which of the cooperative skills from this list did you use?*

In most cases, this exercise will allow students to experience the value of teamwork and to feel more comfortable within the group. If, based on your observations and the discussion following the activity, you feel that students are relatively comfortable with their groups and that groups are ready to take on a curricular task, your team-building is complete. Some behaviors that signal that students are ready to begin curricular work are the following:

- relaxed body language
- friendly facial expressions
- laughter
- interaction that includes all group members
- prolonged discussion

Here are several other team-building activities that are quick (5 to 10 minutes), simple, and fun. You can use them whenever you create new groups for other groupwork activities.

- **Finish That Thought** Ask students to discuss one of the following ideas. These are simple, non-academic ideas that will give them something interesting to discuss to ease the tension of working together. Remind students to use their best listening skills as each student responds to the prompt.

  If I had a million dollars I would...
  I am most proud that I can...
  The funniest thing that ever happened to me was...
  Next year, I will be able to...
  If I were the teacher of this class, I would...
  My very favorite meal is...
  If you walked into my room at home, you'd see...
  The best pet in the world would be...
  My favorite movie is...

- **Team Handshake** Have groups develop a team handshake and share it with the class. This is a special way for students to shake hands to show they belong to a particular group. This quick, kinesthetic task will help bring students together and ease tension.

- **Team Logo** Pass out pieces of butcher paper and have each group design a logo using words, symbols, drawings, and color. The logos should reflect the interests and personalities of the group members. Have groups share their logos with the class.

- **Human Statues** Give each group a different object to form with their bodies, such as a tree, computer, car, table, bicycle, slide, octopus, elephant, or airplane. You may want to award bonus points to groups who can physically represent their object so well that it is immediately identifiable to the class.

- **Famous Person** Have groups choose a famous person to join their group and explain why that person would be a helpful group member for the activity.

- **Best Number** Have groups select a number between 1 and 100 to represent their group. Ask them to give three reasons for their choice.

- **Team Sport** Have students choose a sport to represent their group and tell three ways their group is similar to that sport.

Friendly expressions, laughter, and interaction among all group members are indications that team-building has been successful.

- **Theme Song** Have students select a theme song for their group and perform it for the class.

- **Letter Scramble** Have students combine the letters of their first names to make a phrase or sentence to describe their group.

- **How Much Is Your Group Worth?** Assign each letter of the alphabet a numerical value (Z = 1, Y = 2, X = 3, and so on). Have each group member write his or her first name and compute its numerical value. Then have group members add the individual values to determine a group value. Have groups compare values.

When Use "Going Camping" or "Lost on the Moon" when students are embarking on their first formal groupwork activity, usually during the third, fourth, or fifth week of school. Use the simpler teambuilders whenever you form new groups for subsequent activities.

Going Camping

You are going camping with friends near a mountain lake. The lake is fed by a fast-running stream. You plan to stay five days.

Your friends have already arrived early to set up camp. They have a tent, sleeping bags, food, and a gas stove with plenty of fuel but no way to light it. You must hike three miles to meet them at the lake.

You realize that you can't carry all you planned to bring. So you have to decide what to take.

Your job is to rank the 10 items below from **most important** for camping to **least important** for camping. Place 1 by the most important, 2 by the second most important, and so on. The least important item will be ranked 10.

You will rank these items twice. First, you will rank them on your own (Phase 1). Then you will talk with your group members and rank them again as a group (Phase 2).

Item	Phase 1 Your Ranking	Error Points	Phase 2 Team Ranking	Error Points	Experts' Ranking
A. 5-gallon jug of water					
B. Candy					
C. Clothes					
D. Cooking pot					
E. Fishing pole					
F. Flashlight					
G. Small canteen of water					
H. Matches					
I. Trail map					
J. Bag full of toys					
Total					

Lost on the Moon

Your spaceship has just crash-landed on the lighted side of the moon. You were supposed to meet up with the mother ship 200 miles away on the moon's surface. However, the rough landing has ruined your ship. All equipment on board was destroyed, except for the 15 items listed below.

Your crew's survival depends on reaching the mother ship. You must choose the most critical items for the 200-mile trip. Your task is to rank the 15 items in terms of their importance for survival. Place 1 by the most important item, 2 by the second most important, and so on through 15, the least important.

You will rank these items twice. First you will rank them on your own (Phase 1). You will then consult with your group and rank them again (Phase 2). Share your individual solutions, and agree on a group ranking for each item. NASA experts have determined the best solution. Their answers will be revealed later.

Item	*Phase 1 Your Ranking*	*Error Points Phase 2*	*Team Ranking*	*Error Points*	*NASA's Ranking*
A. Box of matches	______	______	______	______	______
B. Food concentrate	______	______	______	______	______
C. 50 feet of nylon rope	______	______	______	______	______
D. Parachute silk	______	______	______	______	______
E. Solar-powered portable heater	______	______	______	______	______
F. Two pistols	______	______	______	______	______
G. One case of dehydrated milk	______	______	______	______	______
H. Two 100-pound tanks of oxygen	______	______	______	______	______
I. Map of the stars (seen from the moon)	______	______	______	______	______
J. Self-inflating life raft	______	______	______	______	______
K. Magnetic compass	______	______	______	______	______
L. 5 gallons of water	______	______	______	______	______
M. Signal flares	______	______	______	______	______
N. First-aid kit with injection needles	______	______	______	______	______
O. Solar-powered FM receiver-transmitter	______	______	______	______	______
Total	______	______	______	______	______

Experts' Rankings for "Going Camping"

Item	*Experts' Rank*	*Explanation*
A	10	The water jug would be very heavy to carry for three miles. Plus, there's plenty of water that can be boiled for drinking at the campsite.
B	8	There is already food at the campsite, so this is not necessary.
C	5	Clothes beyond what you are already wearing would be helpful for the five-day stay. But being able to get to the campsite, drink water, and eat are more important.
D	4	This is needed for cooking, which is essential.
E	7	Since food is already at the campsite, this is not a critical item. But it is a good source of recreation.
F	6	A light source will be useful at night.
G	2	This is necessary for drinking water along the hike and in case of an accident.
H	3	Matches are essential for lighting the gas stove, which boils drinking water and cooks food.
I	1	Without a trail map, you cannot find your way to the campsite.
J	9	Toys are not essential, and they would be bulky and difficult to carry.

NASA's Rankings for "Lost on the Moon"

Item	*NASA's Rank*	*Explanation*
A	15	Matches are useless. They cannot burn without oxygen.
B	4	You need food. (But you need air and water more.)
C	6	Useful for climbing rock cliffs.
D	8	Offers shelter from the sun.
E	13	Not needed on the lighted side, and won't work on the dark side.
F	11	Use to make a self-propulsion device.
G	12	Bulky and not as useful as food concentrate.
H	1	The most pressing need. You must have oxygen to breathe.
I	3	The best way to find your travel route.
J	9	The CO2 bottle in the raft may be used for propulsion.
K	14	The moon's magnetic field is not polarized; a magnetic compass is useless.
L	2	Replacement for the high loss of body water (from sweating).
M	10	Use as a distress signal when the mother ship is sighted.
N	7	Vitamins and medicines are injected with needles that fit a special opening in the space suits.
O	5	Needed for communication with mother ship.

STEP 9 Allow students to engage in groupwork activities without unnecessary interventions by you.

Rationale One of the main functions of groupwork tasks is to allow students to grapple with new social studies concepts and to learn problem solving skills. Often, teachers are too quick to intervene when students appear stuck. Resist the temptation to solve groups' problems. Instead, allow students to struggle—and perhaps even fail—at a task, provided that you debrief with the group what worked and what didn't so they can learn from the experience.

What to Do Once students have begun working on a groupwork task, it's time for you to step aside and monitor student activity more discreetly. For example, you may want to observe and praise on-task behavior, record group progress for assessment, and note cooperative skills that groups are using. Curb impulses to control group interaction; don't hover around the groups or engage in problem solving. If students ask for substantive help, try to help them figure out how to solve the issue themselves. Accept questions from groups only when all members have raised their hands.

The critical role for you comes after students have finished the groupwork activity. Then it's time for you to lead a discussion focusing on the group process. Center your discussion around these questions:

- How did your group interact?
- Which cooperative skills were exhibited the most?
- What did your group do well?
- What could you have improved?
- If another group of students were to do this same activity, what suggestions would you make?

Allowing groups as much autonomy as possible encourages them to work out problems on their own.

When Use this approach any time students are engaged in groupwork activities.

Discuss key premises behind the TCI Approach with your students.

Rationale Students can become even more active and informed learners if you explain to them the rationale behind your teaching. Students are fascinated and appreciative—especially after they have experienced several activities—when they discover why you are teaching in this manner. The information will help them better understand you, the class, and their own learning styles so that they can benefit even more from this approach.

What to Do After you have finished your first several lessons, reveal to students the key premises of the TCI Approach, as discussed in the introduction to this book. This explanation is crucial for two reasons. First, it informs students of the theories that guide your teaching. More importantly, it validates the academic worth of all class members by pointing out that individuals have diverse abilities and unique talents that make learning together exciting and fun.

Project a transparency of "Key Ideas for Students Behind the TCI Approach" (see opposite page). Discuss each idea with your students, and have them give examples of ways each idea has been acknowledged and addressed in your class.

When Reveal this after students have had at least six weeks' experience with the TCI Approach in your classroom.

Key Ideas for Students Behind the TCI Approach

1. Students have different learning styles.

Each of us is stronger in some types of intelligence than in others.

- You might be "word smart," or have verbal-linguistic intelligence.
- You might be "music smart," or have musical-rhythmic intelligence.
- You might be "number smart," or have logical-mathematical intelligence.
- You might be "picture smart," or have visual-spatial intelligence.
- You might be "body smart," or have body-kinesthetic intelligence.
- You might be "people smart," or have interpersonal intelligence.
- You might be "self-smart," or have intrapersonal intelligence.

2. Cooperative interaction increases learning.

Working in a group helps people

- get along with others.
- solve problems and accomplish goals.
- improve their speaking and listening skills.

3. All students can learn.

Anyone can learn any subject if

- lessons "spiral" from easier ideas to harder ideas.
- harder ideas are discovered step-by-step.

4. Students learn best when they have a clear goal.

Students' understanding improves when

- they know what they will learn and do with their learning.
- their learning is assessed by gathering several forms of evidence.
- there is a plan that identifies how they will reach their goals.

5. Reading and nonreading activities improve learning.

Visual, audio, and movement activities

- help students think about and remember what they've read.
- provide memorable experiences for all types of learners.

PART

3

Using the Interactive Student Notebook

Using the Interactive Student Notebook

"Notebooks have made my students more responsible for their own learning. They have become more involved in the lessons, more attentive during the activities and reading, and more precise in their note taking."

Posted on a wall of almost every elementary classroom in the nation, you will likely see the crowded daily agenda: reading, writing, spelling, math, physical education, science, music, art, and sometimes even social studies. With all the subjects elementary teachers are responsible for covering, it's no wonder social studies is taught so sporadically. Consequently, most elementary students get a fragmented view of the subject. It is difficult for them to remember—much less synthesize and apply—what they learn. And it is almost impossible for teachers to measure student growth. This is why elementary teachers across the nation are turning to Interactive Student Notebooks as a cornerstone of social studies instruction.

Students eagerly take out these notebooks when it is time to begin a social studies lesson. The Interactive Student Notebook provides a cohesive structure and serves as the organizational anchor for the multiple intelligence activities that occur in a TCI lesson. Students' work in the Interactive Student Notebook centers on three key elements of the TCI Approach:

- **Preview Assignments** At the start of a lesson, a short, intriguing assignment helps students connect the upcoming lesson to their own experience, activating their prior knowledge.
- **Graphically Organized Reading Notes** As the lesson unfolds, students use a section called Reading Notes to record, in a striking graphic format, main ideas and supporting details of what they are learning.
- **Processing Assignments** Students end the lesson with a Processing assignment —perhaps involving an illustrated timeline, matrix, annotated map, flowchart, advertisement, or persuasive letter—to synthesize and apply their learning.

Examples of each of these parts of the notebook can be found in the corresponding sections of this book.

Help Students to See the Coherent Whole

The Interactive Student Notebook groups assignments by lesson, so that students can see a logical flow from assignment to assignment. Their notebooks serve as a chronological record of their work and help reinforce the major concepts and themes.

Why Interactive Student Notebooks Engage Students

Teachers find that their students embrace the Interactive Student Notebook enthusiastically. "I used to hate taking notes and filling out worksheets in class," one student commented, "but I love working on my notebook because it's fun." Teachers also report that because the Interactive Student Notebook encourages a variety of forms of expression, there's more interest and more involvement by students, in addition to more learning and better retention. Here's why Interactive Student Notebooks truly engage students:

They reach out to students, inviting them to be active participants in their learning. Many students are accustomed to filling out blanks on a worksheet or laboriously copying teacher-written notes from the board or the overhead. The Interactive Student Notebook changes that. At the beginning of a lesson, students are "hooked" with a personalized Preview assignment that taps into their own experiences and prior knowledge. Then students are encouraged to record Reading Notes accurately for a *purpose*—searching for implications or assumptions, identifying main ideas, providing supporting details, interpreting information. They will use this information during Processing assignments that challenge them to really *think* and apply what they have learned. As a result, students become more creative, more independent thinkers.

"Students like that the notebooks allow them the freedom and creativity to express themselves in a variety of ways. Parents continually tell me that they think it's fantastic that kids are relating social studies to their lives and writing about what they learn in their notebooks."

They encourage students to use a variety of intelligences, not just linguistic intelligence. Conventional student notebooks may work for motivated students with strong linguistic skills, but they do not work as well for students with other predominant intelligences. In the Interactive Student Notebook, students approach understanding in many ways. They can tap into their *visual* intelligence through such elements as graphs, maps, illustrations, pictowords, and visual metaphors; their *musical* intelligence by composing song lyrics or reacting to a piece of music; their *intrapersonal* intelligence by reflecting on the ways social studies topics affect them personally; their *interpersonal* intelligence by recording group discussions and group project notes; and their *logical-mathematical* intelligence through sequencing and the use of spectrums, graphs, and charts.

Spotlight Student Notebooks

Showcase exceptional notebooks so students have the opportunity to gather ideas for improving their own notebooks. You might set up six or eight stations around the class-room, put an exceptional notebook at each, and conduct a "gallery walk." Allow students 15 or 20 minutes to roam around the room and collect ideas from the model notebooks.

They help students to organize systematically as they learn. Students use their notebooks to record ideas about every social studies lesson. They use a variety of organizational techniques—topic headings, color-coding, different writing styles—to give coherence to what they learn. The notebook also helps students keep assignments together and in a logical order. Gone are the days of notes and assignments wadded up and stuffed in backpacks or lockers.

They become a portfolio of individual learning. These personal, creative notebooks become a record of each student's growth. Teachers, students, and even family members can review a student's progress in writing, thinking, and organizational skills. This makes them useful for parent conferences.

Hints for Making Effective Interactive Student Notebooks

Teachers use the Interactive Student Notebook in a variety of forms. Some give their students the consumable workbook that is provided with TCI's core program materials. Teachers who elect to use this consumable can follow the sequence exactly as designed, having students complete the specified Previews, Reading Notes, and Processing assignments. This helps teachers who are new to the TCI Approach, since they can rely on the published Interactive Student Notebook for support while they are learning to use the essential elements and strategies of the program.

Other teachers elect to supplement the printed workbook with their own handouts and materials that students bring in. Students use spiral-bound notebooks, clasp folders, or three-ring binders to combine the materials, cutting and pasting as they create their own unique Interactive Student Notebooks. In this format, TCI materials serve as the backbone, but teachers have the flexibility to tailor instruction to suit their needs.

Still other teachers may be developing their own curricular materials based on the TCI Approach. They won't have a published notebook to start with, but they can follow the same structure, having students create spiral-bound Interactive Student Notebooks that include the teacher's own prereading or Preview activities, graphic organizers for capturing content notes, and Processing assignments, plus any additional support materials. Creating this type of Interactive Student Notebook is labor-intensive, but many teachers are willing and eager to take on the task because of the tremendous success of this powerful organizational and instructional tool.

Regardless of the format you plan to use, the following hints will increase the effectiveness of your Interactive Student Notebooks and allow students' individual styles to flourish.

1. Supply materials that inspire creativity. An abundance of materials—colored pencils and markers, scissors, glue sticks, colored highlighters—will spark creativity for notebook assignments. Some teachers keep a class set of such materials in their room for in-class work on the notebooks.

Students use their visual intelligence when they interpret information graphically in their notebooks. With colored markers and construction paper, they create vivid images that help them understand and remember key concepts.

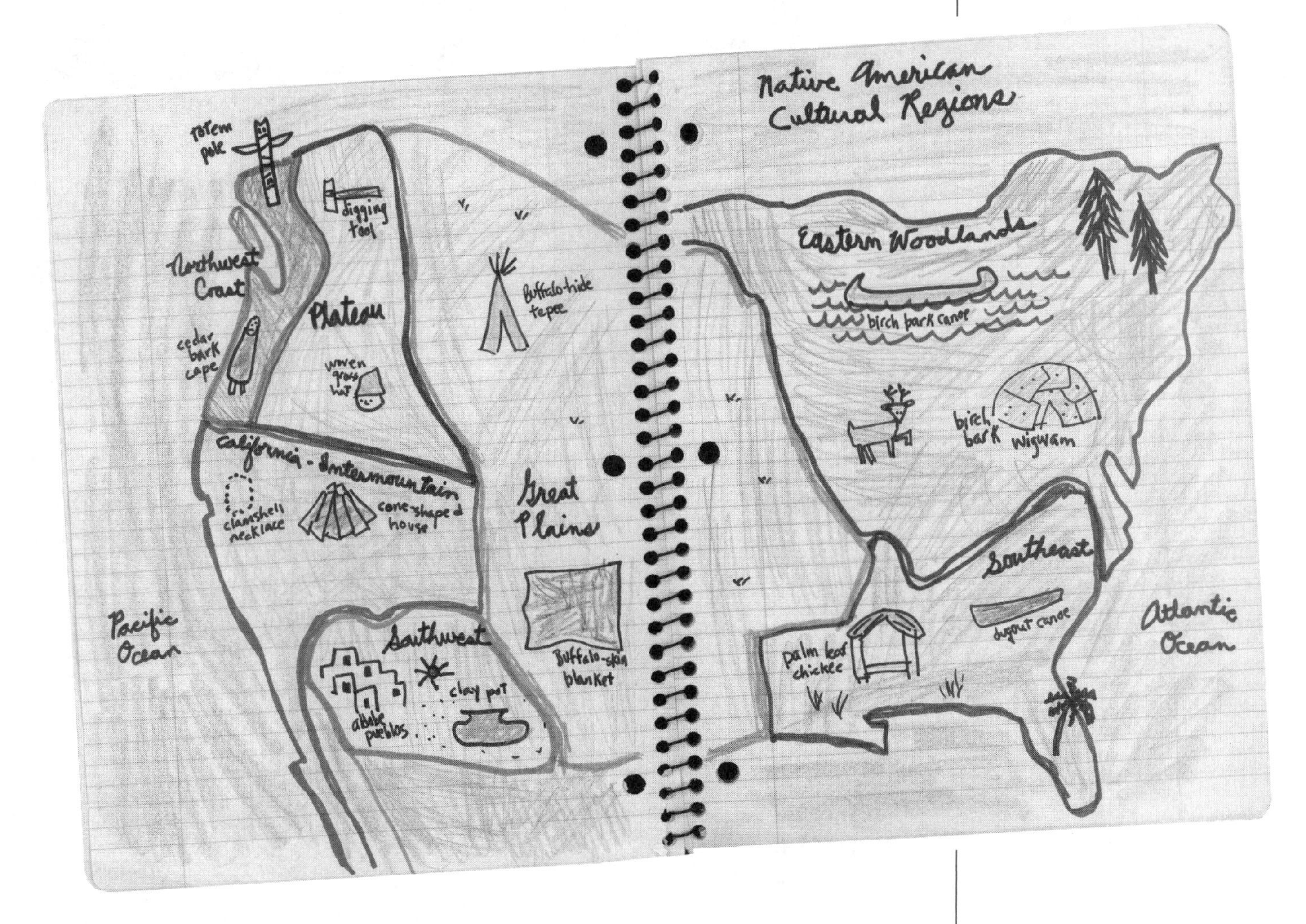

2. Let students create their own covers. When you introduce the Interactive Student Notebook, encourage students to embellish theirs with a colorful cover that in some way reflects the content you are teaching. This immediately sends students the message that the notebooks will be their own creations that they can take pride in—and it helps cut down on the number of lost notebooks during the year.

Notebook covers can be as individual as your students. It's up to you to specify which information you consider essential for the cover, such as the subject area, student's name, classroom, teacher's name, or date.

3. Personalize the notebooks with an author page. Have students create a page about themselves to include at the front of their notebooks. Their author page could include a portrait or photograph, as well as personal information or favorite quotes. (As needed, remind students that any content unsuitable at school is also unacceptable for use in notebooks.) With both a personalized cover and an author page, very few notebooks get lost.

4. Consider adding a table of contents. The consumable workbook format comes with a simple table of contents. If students are assembling their own notebooks, you may want them to create a running table of contents. This helps them stay organized and ensures that they have a record of all assignments. Ideally, all of their social studies work is collected in the notebook, so they will list the Preview, Reading and Activity Notes, and Processing for every lesson.

Lost Notebooks?

Because students take a great deal of pride of ownership in their notebooks, typically very few are lost during a semester. Most teachers report that only a handful of students lose them each year. If your students do lose their notebooks, consider allowing them to make up a select number of assignments so they may receive partial credit.

Table of Contents

Social Studies Classroom Rules	p.1
M.I. Name Activity	p.2,3
Prereading Chapter One	p.4-5
Preview Chapter One	p.6
Vocabulary Chapter One	p.7
World map, Continents and Oceans	p.9
Map 2 Latitude & Longitude	p.13-14
Ocean & Continents	p.11-12
Map 3 Geography terms	p.15-16
Map 4 Physical features	p.17-18
Pre-Reading Chapter Two	p.19
Vocabulary Chapter 2	p.21-22
Pre-view Chapter Two	p.21
Reading notes Chapter two	p.22
Pre reading Chapter 3	p.23
Vocabulary Chapter 3	p.25
Preview Chapter 3	p.27
Reading notes Chapter 3	
R.N. Ch Four	
Prereading Chapter Five	
Vocabulary Ch 5	
Reading Questions and answer	
Reading Notes	
Prereading Ch 6	
Vocabulary Ch 6	

DATE	ASSIGNMENT	PAGE	POINTS
11-14	preview 6 southeast	39	9/10
11-15	geography challenge 6	40	7/10
11-16	map of southeast	42	10/10
11-17	tour site 3 Jamestown	43	8/10
11-18	tour site 6 riverboat	44	10/10
11-21	tour site 9 Montgomery	45	9/10
11-23	letter about the trip	46	10/10
11-30	Preview 7 climate	48	10/10
12-1	notes on placards	49	8/10
12-6	Processing 7	53	10/10

A contents page for the notebook helps students stay organized. It can be as simple as a list of assignments and the page where each can be found. These examples show two possible formats. Recording the scores for individual assignments will help you immensely when it's time to grade the notebook as a whole.

It Takes Time

Teaching students how to use Interactive Student Notebooks is a complex task. It takes patience, good modeling, and constant reinforcement. Your students' notebooks will improve dramatically over time.

5. Give clear guidelines for the notebooks. One of the most important steps for successful notebooks is to establish clear guidelines. Decide ahead of time what you expect your students to produce in their notebooks, and then clearly communicate your expectations. Most teachers create a list of criteria on which notebooks will be graded and have students attach it to the inside cover of the notebook.

You might also send a letter to students and families, explaining the purpose of the notebook and your expectations. See, for example, the sample guidelines shown opposite. Note that this teacher uses the consumable workbook for blackline masters. Students glue these worksheets into a spiral notebook, interspersed with their own work.

How to Manage Interactive Student Notebooks

With daily assignments to review and grade for each student in three to four other content areas besides social studies, you will need a simple system for assessing these notebooks. Ideally, you will both informally assess the notebooks on a regular basis, to give students immediate feedback, and also formally collect and grade the notebooks every three to four weeks. The assessment section of this book offers tips for managing the assessment of student notebooks.

Create an "Interactive *Teacher* Notebook." One very useful management tool is a master notebook in which you record each notebook assignment, attach student handouts, store copies of content notes, and make annotations on the activities for future reference—notes on how they went, which groups or individuals seemed to have trouble with them and why, and what questions really worked to prompt good critical thinking. By keeping a master notebook, you have a visual record of what took place in class.

The Interactive Student Notebook helps make learning social studies an enjoyable, interactive, successful experience. Teachers are often surprised and thrilled by their students' enthusiasm for the subject.

The Interactive Teacher Notebook serves both the teacher and the students. For the teacher, this tool

- functions as the teacher's lesson-planning book.
- includes a table of contents that becomes the "official" record of assignments.
- provides a place to store extra materials and handouts.
- communicates special instructions for students who have been absent.
- serves as a journal to reflect on the effectiveness of activities and assignments and ways to improve them.

For students, the Interactive Teacher Notebook

- is a place they can find any information and assignments they missed during an absence.
- serves as a model of how assignments should be title, dated, and arranged.
- allows them to check the completeness of their own notebook.

Interactive Student Notebook Guidelines

What is the purpose of the Interactive Notebook?

The purpose is to help you be a creative, independent thinker.
Your notebook will be used for taking notes on your social studies reading, and sometimes on the activities we do in class. You will express your ideas and apply what you have learned.

What materials do I need?

- Spiral notebook (white paper, college-ruled, at least 100 pages)
- Blue and black pens, number 2 pencil
- Glue stick and scissors
- Colored pens and pencils, highlighters

What goes in my notebook?

Everything we do in social studies. It will contain your reading notes, written assignments, maps, diagrams, and artwork.

How will my notebook be graded?

I will look for these things:

- Is your notebook complete? Have you finished all the assignments?
- What is the quality of your work?
- Is your notebook well organized?
- Is your notebook NEAT and attractive? Have you included drawings?

I will check the notebooks from time to time—usually every 3 or 4 weeks. All class notes and notebook assignments must be included, even for days you were absent.

What happens if I am absent?

If you are absent, it is your responsibility to get the notebook assignments from a classmate or from the teacher.

Please share this handout with your parent or guardian. When both of you have read this information, please sign your names below.

Student Signature ______________________________

Parent Signature ______________________________

References

Armbruster, Bonnie B. 1984. The problem of "inconsiderate text." In G. G. Duffy, L. R. Roehler, and J. Mason (Eds.), *Comprehension Instruction: Perspectives and Suggestions*. New York: Longman.

Berger, Joseph, Susan Rosenholtz, and Morris Zelditch, Jr. 1980. Status organizing processes. *Annual Review of Sociology* 6: 479–508.

Billmeyer, Rachel. 1996. *Teaching Reading in the Content Areas: If Not Me, Then Who?* Aurora, CO: Mid-continent Regional Educational Laboratory.

Bruner, Jerome. 1960. *The Process of Education*. Cambridge, MA: Harvard University Press.

Center for Civic Education. 1997. *National Standards of Civics and Government*. Calabasas, CA.

Cohen, Elizabeth. 1986. *Designing Groupwork: Strategies for the Heterogeneous Classroom*. New York: Columbia University Teachers College.

Gardner, Howard. 1993. *Frames of Mind: The Theory of Multiple Intelligences*. 10th anniversary edition. New York: Basic Books.

Harvey, Stephanie. 1998. *Nonfiction Matters: Reading, Writing, and Research in Grades 3–8*. Portland, ME: Stenhouse.

Keene, Ellen O. and Susan Zimmermann. 1997. *Mosaic of Thought: Teaching Comprehension in a Reader's Workshop*. Portsmouth, NH: Heinemann.

Kinsella, Kate. 2001. Using expository text with fifth graders. *In History Alive! America's Past: User's Guide*. Palo Alto, CA: Teachers' Curriculum Institute.

Marzano, Robert J., Debra J. Pickering, and Jane E. Pollock. 2001. *Classroom Instruction That Works: Research-based Strategies for Increasing Student Achievement*. Alexandria, VA: Association for Supervision and Curriculum Development.

National Association of Colleges and Employees (NACE). 2002. "Job Outlook 2003 Survey of Employers." Bethlehem, PA: NACE.

National Council for the Social Studies. 1984. Social studies for young children. NCSS Position Statement prepared by Elementary/Early Childhood Education Committee. Retrieved January 20, 2005, from http://www.socialstudies.org/positions/children/

Newmann, Fred M., Joseph Onosko, and Robert B. Stevenson. 1990. Staff development for higher-order thinking: A synthesis of practical wisdom. *Journal of Staff Development* 11(3): 48–55.

Ogle, Donna. 1986. K-W-L: A teaching model that develops active reading of expository text. *The Reading Teacher* 39: 564–570.

Parker, Walter C. 2001. *Social Studies in Elementary Education*, 11th ed. Upper Saddle River, NJ: Merrill Prentice Hall.

Pearson, P. David, L. R. Roehler, J. A. Dole, and G. G. Duffy. 1992. Developing expertise in reading comprehension. In S. J. Samuels and A. E. Farstrup (Eds.), *What Research Has to Say About Reading Instruction*. Newark, DE: International Reading Association.

Shulman, Judith H., Rachel A. Lotan, and Jennifer A. Whitcomb (Eds.). 1998. *Groupwork in Diverse Classrooms: A Casebook for Educators*. New York: Teachers College Press.

Tierney, R. J., J. E. Readance, and E. K. Dishner. 1995. *Reading Strategies and Practices: A Compendium*. 4th ed. Needham Heights, MA: Allyn and Bacon

Wiggins, Grant and Jay McTighe. 2005. *Understanding by Design*. Arlington, VA: Association for Supervision and Curriculum Development.

Credits

19, North Wind Picture Archives; **20,** © Will and Deni McIntyre/Corbis; **25,** Len Ebert; **26, upper,** Corbis; **26, middle,** Getty Images/PhotoDisc; **27,** Renata Lohman; **28, lower,** North Wind Picture Archives; **32, upper, Corbis; 32,** lower, Corbis; **33,** Library of Congress; **56, upper,** Library of Congress; **56, lower,** Library of Congress; **57,** © Mike Kowalski/Illustration Works, Inc.; **63,** Doug Roy; **95,** Culver Pictures; **104,** Doug Roy; **106,** Doug Roy